Giving Light to Darkness

Giving Light to Darkness

A TRUE STORY OF THE DEBILITATING CONTROL OF POST CONCUSSION SYNDROME DEPRESSION

LAURA KIMBRO

ISBN: 978-1-958150-12-2
Giving Light to Darkness: A true story of the debilitating control of post concussion syndrome depression

Paperpack
July 2022

Subjects:
PSYCHOLOGY / Psychopathology / Depression
FAMILY & RELATIONSHIPS / Death, Grief, Bereavement
HEALTH & FITNESS / Diseases & Conditions / Nervous System (incl. Brain)

Published by Inner Peace Press
Eau Claire, Wisconsin, USA
www.innerpeacepress.com

I share the white heart and the white dove and the inner sunset because Seth's favorite color was sunset orange and the day of his services there was just the most beautiful amazing sunset it seemed that sunset lingered in the days that followed, so now anytime there's an amazing sunset... we like to say he sure does paint the sky beautiful.

It is real.

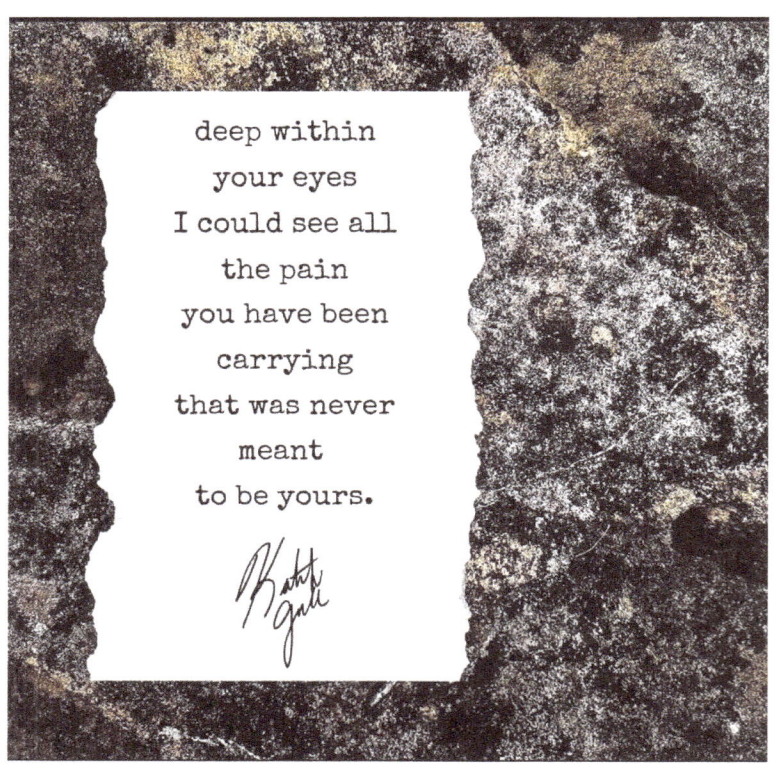

deep within
your eyes
I could see all
the pain
you have been
carrying
that was never
meant
to be yours.

TABLE OF CONTENTS

At a restaurant after the accident, with mouth wired shut

Dedication

MY HEART KNEW... THE minute I got to you, the minute your soul spoke to mine… My heart knew the pain that knocked you to your knees and deceived your mind.

You fought so hard and for so long, my heart knew you just got tired of the battle that had now crept inside.

Seth Michael I know you... my son ~the real you~ you only meant to be gone for a while, to quiet this storm that sought you… you were coming back when the winds died down, you were just seeking cover… I would have thrown you a life raft, I would have sheltered you with my sails. I'm so sorry sweet boy, I'm so, so sorry.

I looked to the sky for days, for months, in what felt like eternity… I raised my hands… I asked God, "Why?!?!" I fell to my knees. I wanted to curse him. I wanted to abandon him just as he abandoned you…

But then I became still and my heart knew… he's held you every step of the way...

When he picked me to be your mom and I got to love you and I got to protect you, I got to watch you grow from a little boy to the man you became. I got you for 24 years. No, it wasn't enough time, but it was long enough to last forever.

My heart knows our souls still connect, our body is only our vessel. I carried you... that's my heart, that's my soul's connection to yours!!

Death cannot steal that from me... you are mine and I am yours... my grief is just my unconditional love for you with nowhere to go.

I now raise my hands to the sky. I thank God he gave me you, I thank God I got to be your mom. I thank God your life was spared that day, I thank God you got 22 more months.

My heart has learned we're never promised tomorrow. My heart has learned God only promises us life and death... it's our expectation and human arrogance that we feel entitled to 80!!

My heart knows God and, just as I, he too has always loved you and protected you. When death sought you... he saved you. He gave you back to me... You got to make future plans, you got to feel an endless love from a beautiful soul mate, you got to love her for the rest of your life and she yours.

This is my hard "unfinished journey," the next chapter of life for you...

As hours without you turned into days... days into months... and now months into a year. And then more...

My heart knew why you weren't here... you're bigger than this life, you're meant to still do great things you've always had the Heart of a Hero and through you and our knowledge you will and can change lives... this my heart knows!

Until we meet again above the stars, my beautiful boy with a contagious laugh and eyes that smile, I'll be loving you heart to heart, soul to soul.

~ Love, Mom

He made broken look
beautiful
And strong look
invincible
He walked with the
universe
on his shoulders and
made it look like a
pair of wings

Introduction

I KNOW NOTHING ABOUT writing a book, but I do know our hearts and what I hope to convey to the world about us, our son, and his life…

Early on, within a month of our son leaving this world, we began our search into what could possibly make someone take their life, to just leave this world, to leave their life and those they love and the people who loved them… what could possibly make him leave in the middle of a song?

His book of life still had many chapters. Seth had a million reasons to live.

His leaving just didn't make sense, I felt we were hit by a hurricane. "What just actually happened to our lives?!" Post concussion syndrome is what happened!! It is known as the "silent killer" of injuries.

As I started researching, I began to understand just what crept into our son's mind and played havoc on his very soul. Seth wasn't looking to leave this world, he just didn't understand what he didn't know… he'd look in the mirror but wasn't seeing his pre-injury self any more. He felt like a stranger in his own body.

I now know many facts and statistics on suicide and concussion. I also know my son. In this book I'll share some very vital information on how concussion can debilitate you and leave you feeling in great despair.

It's crazy to me how known, yet unknown, this all really is and the silence that surrounds it. I couldn't believe that so many people have some knowledge of what traumatic brain injury (TBI) or post concussion syndrome (PCS) is, but it's only when I go into great detail of the seriousness it causes that people are just blown away by the reality of the illness and the lasting effects it can actually have on a person.

Awareness about the impact of TBI/PCS must be made a top priority to patients as well as family and friends.

Post Traumatic Stress Disorder (PTSD) is something else that needs more attention. PTSD is where my mind first went after the death of our son, for he had just shared with us two days prior to his death of "remembering" his accident.

He was recalling how he threw his hand up (which makes sense to why his wrist was broken). He didn't go into great detail, but he was remembering before his face made contact and he blacked out. I think people view PTSD as a military problem, it's not. Any traumatic event can leave you experiencing PTSD.

I have no doubt our son would still be alive had we known and understood the severity of the TBI/PCS. He'd never had to wonder what was wrong with him and we would have gotten help so much sooner.

This is why I created this book – to bring awareness to this very serious issue.

My purpose is to give light in this darkness. If someone has sustained a TBI or concussion, I want them to know all the facts about what can happen even months or years in the future. They might start feeling helpless, angered, emotionally withdrawn, or just questioning their own worth. Know this is part of the injury… you're not going crazy. And there is help, you are not alone!!

Don't let TBI/PCS depression continue as "a silent killer." Pay attention to the "walking wounded" ~ so we don't have to bear one more victim of its grip.

A Mother's Heart

I've been playing this in my mind and heart. Living it daily over the last almost nine months. 4/17/22

Last time Dad and I spent nine months without our son I was carrying him all safe and tucked away within me. This month's 17th date will be hard... it's those little things that are so big in a mother's mind. It's things I'm sure the rest of the world doesn't think about unless you've lost a child. I spent my children's whole lives protecting them... always had eyes and ears on them, always felt blessed they were mine and I was theirs... never thought I'd need to protect them from themselves. Post concussion syndrome depression is like a thief in the night... it came, it destroyed, and it killed.

Recognizing the ninth month weighed heavy in my thoughts of not having him here. I realize there will be these monumental days that will cut me to my core. This evening I felt his presence as we lit up the night sky for him with lanterns. There was a glow that was fluttering quickly around us, and it showed up in a few videos I took of the lanterns. I took a screenshot to look at it still and saw that it was actually white, and looked like an Angel. I choose to believe he sends his love in all ways possible.

Since his journey home I've been more intrigued by sunrises and sunsets. I guess for me it's in their beauty and it's the closest to heaven we get. Even as the moon began to make its appearance in the night sky that evening, there was the most beautiful casting around it. I couldn't help but say out loud "there's an Angel." I just couldn't believe what I was seeing — I didn't care if I sounded crazy... I could see it and in that moment I took my camera to the sky.

Within a few months of his absence, I needed to share with his friends and family what we were beginning to unravel and understand. Everyone had questions — they too needed to know "what just happened"?? So I began to write in hopes to bring some clarity to what Seth was going through.

It's taken me some time to gather all our emotions and knowledge and to put them into words to share with you all, but here is our message for his friends and family.

I've spent the last 174 days just trying to piece this all together. 174 days since we've heard your voice, seen you, hugged you, and what started out as three months has now turned into eight months since we lost you — we lost us! Our son, our friend, our brother, our fiancé.

I come to you all now to try my best to give some light on the darkness that Seth faced that night... it doesn't take it all away or make it right, it just gives some answers to everyone's questions of "how" and "why."

Seth was suffering from TBI/PCS (traumatic brain injury/post concussion syndrome) depression. This depression is a silent killer, an inner battle many suffer after a traumatic injury, which Seth endured September 1, 2019. Although Seth miraculously lived through the accident... His injuries were much more than just his jaw being broken in "three" separate places and his chin shattered and missing teeth... he was living with a much deeper wound: the battle of TBI/PCS depression.

You may wonder ~ what is TBI/PCS depression? It is called a "silent killer" that goes largely unnoticed among the walking wounded of head injuries... It's caused by a blow or blunt force trauma/traumatic jolt to the head/face/skull... Seth's injuries were very traumatic. His face had come in contact with a DFO (deadly fixed object) structure. There were two mailboxes inside of an indestructible casing that was concreted into the ground and made of unforgiving material!

At the time we felt so blessed that Seth survived the accident. Doctors had said it was a miracle!! Little did he or we realize the effects the TBI/PCS would plague in his mind over the next 22 months. He looked mended on the outside, but in his head he was struggling. You could say, "Seth made Broken look Beautiful." As his family, we vow to our son to bring more awareness to such a debilitating illness and to the specifications and guidelines of mailbox structures/posts!!

Seth loved life. He was on the upside of the tragic accident he had endured and met a wonderful girl who planned on spending the rest of her life with him. He'd even written out his vows. He'd just started back with Teams, a company he really enjoyed working for. He was getting to have lunch breaks with his dad. Life was just starting to give back to him. So what the hell just happened?

Seth was a great guy with a big heart, he'd do anything for anyone. He was our son, a brother, and an uncle — Lola would call him "her us." Seth had dreams. He had a beautiful life to live!!!

I just know him. And I know Seth didn't even realize what was going on inside his own mind... The real Seth never would have left us all this way.

Sooo many of you asked, just like we asked, "Why? Why now??" Well, that is just what TBI/PCS depression will do. It will plague you, making you feel at your lowest and questioning your own worth!! This has all been so hard, to wrap our heads and hearts around him being gone. He had a whole bright future ahead of him... we had made it through the worst, or so we had thought...

I told him that night, as I knelt down beside him in his garage and held him, "I'll need answers if you want us to make it through this horrific nightmare." I felt his presence telling me, "Mom, I didn't mean this!"

But unfortunately it was all too late. I couldn't fix this, all we could do was helplessly hold him and just give him peace.

Now I talk so Seth can be heard and he's not just the boy "who took his life." He had sooo much to look forward to. Seth loved life... his true self would have chosen to live!!!

Looking through a few conversations on Seth's phone... we have our answers to the darkness Seth faced that night. Over the last few months he had written of being depressed, about his insecurities, just "not feeling the same since his accident," and not fully understanding why he felt this turmoil inside. Well... he just ran ahead of us all for now. 💔

So I'm asking his brothers, his family, to help us spread the word about TBI/PCS depression. Help Seth's voice to be heard and **Please, Please,** people, Follow the Specifications and Regulations of building a Mailbox (by USPS and AASHTO guidelines/standards). ~IT SHOULD BREAK AWAY!!~

Seth had a life... he wanted to live, he really did.

We can be his Voice and Raise more Awareness to All the above!!! Maybe someone you know or love has been in a traumatic accident, or has had a Concussion... know the signs, reach out, talk to them ... let them know it's real....it's not just in their head!!!! Just because there's no brain damage, doesn't mean there's no Brain Injury... it's real and it messes with your psyche!!

We love you son. We'll bare the cross you carried until our last breath. In the near future we would like to plan an event to raise more awareness of TBI/PCS depression to help others who have been in an accident or who have suffered from a concussion~ your feelings of despair are real.. it's not just in your mind!!

Loving you always Seth Michael Kimbro sunrise 5/13/97 to sunset 7/17/21~ until we meet again above the stars.

We're all in this together. I thought if we were going to lose him it would have been right after the accident. Not almost two years later when he was getting better. Who knew that his brain would wreak havoc on him so many months later.

I'm sharing a lot of pictures in this book to show you Seth's transformation. There are pictures of him he had posted a few months after his accident when he was getting his physical strength back by working out. You can see he was starting to feel good about himself as he was posting pictures with his shirt off. Now, taking a closer look through pictures, I can see "the change" as it was taking place. He started losing his confidence. In May they went to Florida and he was wearing his shirt most of the time, even when in the ocean. I piece this together with notes I found he'd written of feeling like complete shit (questioning "why he fucking hates himself"). This all two to three months prior to ending his life.

September 2019 ~ the Accident
April 2021 ~ move in with Fiancé
        (when difficult thoughts started hitting him)
        Started reaching out, not feeling same
July 2021 ~ he ends the battle

Dad and Son

Seth and his beloved niece Lola

Hillory and Seth - Carrying her
in the days ahead

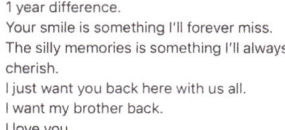

1 year difference.
Your smile is something I'll forever miss.
The silly memories is something I'll always
cherish.
I just want you back here with us all.
I want my brother back.
I love you.

Seth with Lola and Kristin;
Lexi shares her feelings about
missing her brother

About Seth

Seth was our son, a boy with a contagious laugh and a million reasons to live. He had dreams and goals. One of them was a "rugged motorcycle ride" he was planning to take with his dad. Their plan was to take nothing but the clothes on their backs and a backpack. He was planning to take over the bike his dad had customized and dad was getting a new one. They had just spoken of this "rugged ride" two days prior to Seth's leaving. I passively told them we'd all have to plan a big ride together (he, his dad, his fiancé Kristin, and me). Seth spoke up very quickly with a smile saying his dad's and his ride was first.

Seth enjoyed his rides. He rode proudly and free like the wind... we actually came across a video he recorded just the week of July 17... you can feel the freedom he felt. He loved to talk about a ride he and his dad once took together. It involved "splitting the road" (I have to say I wasn't too happy about that) however they smiled and now it makes for a great story.

His life sure was cut short of all the stories still to be written. Seth loved adventures and the outdoors. You could just see he was one with nature. It started as a young kid; he and a few buddies would go into the woods and set up camp... making forts and building a fire. I never worried about him while he was growing up; he was always in the neighborhood scouting... Looking back now, his last comments to me make sense, just wanting to be back young again to "those days..." He wasn't understanding this new concussion brain ~ it was slowly playing havoc on him.

Seth had many passions, and cooking was one of them. He could create anything and loved to show off this skill – he made the best ham subs with just the right seasonings to even more lavish meals like grilled salmon.

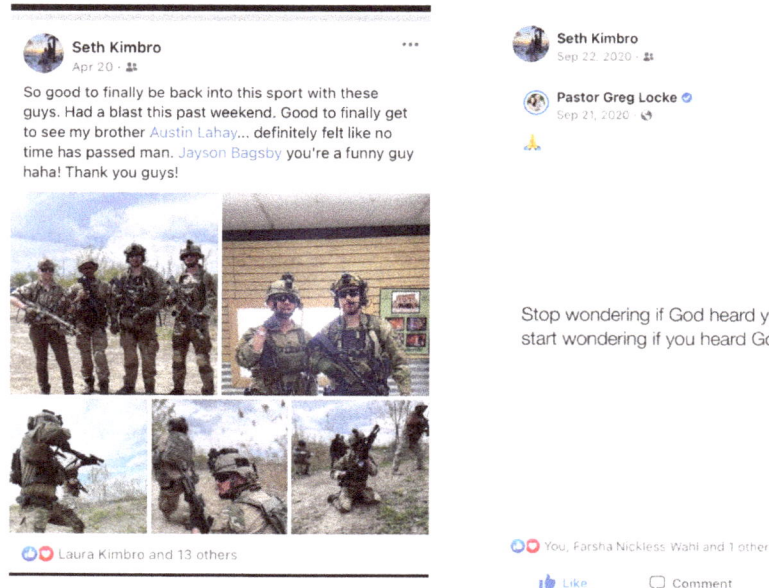

Seth Kimbro
Apr 20 ·

So good to finally be back into this sport with these guys. Had a blast this past weekend. Good to finally get to see my brother Austin Lahay... definitely felt like no time has passed man. Jayson Bagsby you're a funny guy haha! Thank you guys!

Laura Kimbro and 13 others

Seth enjoyed playing Airsoft with his buddies

Seth Kimbro
Sep 22, 2020 ·

Pastor Greg Locke ✓
Sep 21, 2020 ·

🙏

Stop wondering if God heard you and start wondering if you heard God.

You, Farsha Nickless Wahl and 1 other

👍 Like   💬 Comment   ↪ Share

Seth always had a strong belief in God

28

Seth loved being an Uncle

Seth Kimbro
Jun 5, 2020 ·

Mom you're phenomenal! You do a lot for your husband, you're always by his side helping him with anything. You're so supportive to Hillory's, Alexis, and my goals and dreams in life. You go above and beyond for all of us. The mental focus you have on your family goes far beyond just dedication. You have made a legacy of yourself by being the best damn women in this world. So when the day is hard, and you feel overwhelmed just know that you are appreciated, and loved deeply by all of us. So thank you for all that you do for us. We love you!

Laura Kimbro
Charles Kimbro
Hillory Kimbro
Alexis Lynn

You, Laura Kimbro and 27 others   8 Comments

Seth often showed his appreciation

Lexi and Seth during a special moment

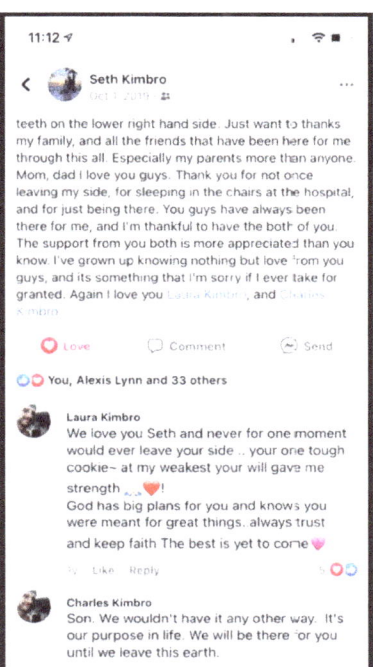

11:12

Seth Kimbro
Oct 1, 2019 ·

teeth on the lower right hand side. Just want to thanks my family, and all the friends that have been here for me through this all. Especially my parents more than anyone. Mom, dad I love you guys. Thank you for not once leaving my side, for sleeping in the chairs at the hospital, and for just being there. You guys have always been there for me, and I'm thankful to have the both of you. The support from you both is more appreciated than you know. I've grown up knowing nothing but love from you guys, and its something that I'm sorry if I ever take for granted. Again I love you Laura Kimbro, and Charles Kimbro

Love   Comment   Send

You, Alexis Lynn and 33 others

Laura Kimbro
We love you Seth and never for one moment would ever leave your side .. your one tough cookie~ at my weakest your will gave me strength ... !
God has big plans for you and knows you were meant for great things. always trust and keep faith The best is yet to come

Like Reply

Charles Kimbro
Son. We wouldn't have it any other way. It's our purpose in life. We will be there for you until we leave this earth.

Seth had a special bond with his family

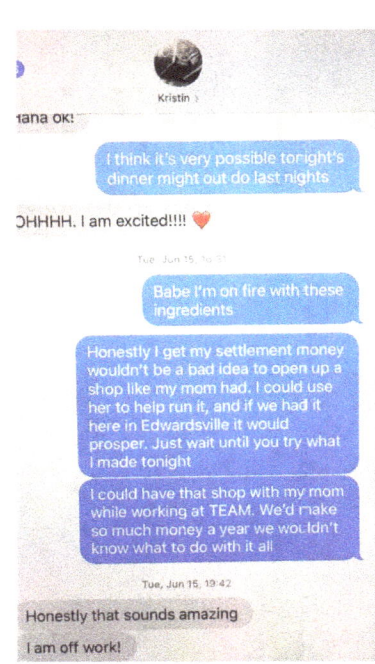

Seth had big dreams

He'd say "I'm on fire with these recipe." He could seriously conjure up anything! He talked of one day having a small restaurant/coffee shop and he would include me in this brilliant idea.

Seth made a journal of plans and dreams he had. He wrote of having a country house with a wrap-around porch and a horse or two... he shared this dream with his love Kristin, he'd make good work of the day then he and she would retreat in the evening by an outdoor fire.

He spoke of his love for Kristin to me many times. He'd say, "Momma, she's the one." And "You ought to hear her when she sings – it's the voice of an Angel." He'd written out his wedding vows with his whole heart and soul. He had saved plans even down to the cost of a trip to Bora Bora for them. There would be two weddings this year, his

28 likes

country_kimbro Well gents today the love of my life said yes to the biggest question of my life! I love you

own and his older sister's. Seth always loved to be a part of things that were of importance to others and he was looking forward to his sister's big day just as much as his own.

His sister was his very first best friend; he knew no matter what happened in life, he could call on her in the good and the bad... she'd always be there. She was four years older than he was and to her he was her "young grasshopper."

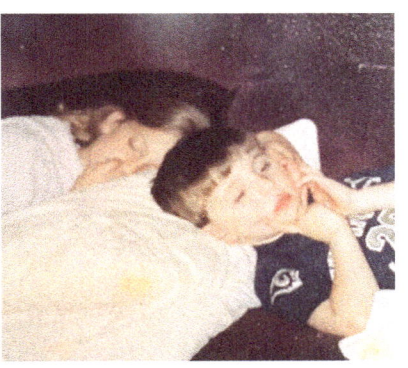

Hillory and Seth - the young grasshopper connection

Seth didn't want to leave his life… he just wanted this battle that crept in to stop… he just didn't understand what was happening. He was beginning to feel disconnected to his own self (life).

Seth has always had somewhat of an old soul and was very patriotic. Since he was a young boy playing with toy soldiers he'd always said he wanted to join the military but as he got older there were things he'd agree and disagree with when it came to war and military ~ fighting for what's right and just. He couldn't conceive taking innocent lives.

Any time he'd come across a veteran he'd pay his respects by paying for their meal or just taking off his hat and shaking their hand, thanking them for their service.

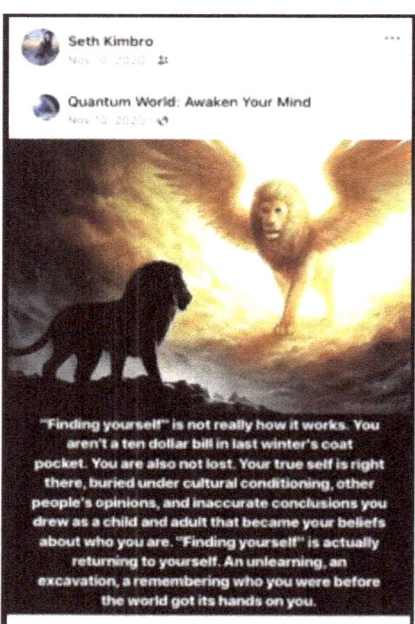

Seth was a deep thinker

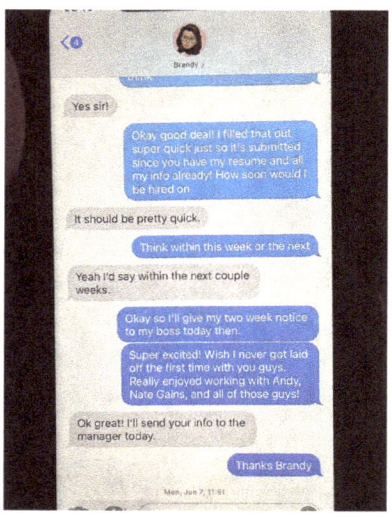

Seth was ready to work

People of all ages enjoyed lengthy conversations with him; many loved his advice and his theories. One theory that still makes me smile: he always had his own thoughts as to if our earth was round or flat and he could give a very good explanation for why it could be flat… guess now he knows the real answer. He was just very intrigued about things like that. Many have said although he was young he had the heart of an old soul.

Seth was always trying to give and be protective of his sisters. He'd give anyone the shirt off his back; there was a time with his younger sister (I think he saw her struggles of being a young mom and just wanted to help her)… he'd given her his truck to help make her life a little easier as

From his phone - his own feelings, where he was at

He circled these - he relied on God for the light

she had a car, but it had some issues and she was living on her own. He was proud of her for being a young mom and trying to do her best, afterall she gave him a sweet niece, Lola who couldn't pronounce Seth so she'd just call him "us." He was just really getting to enjoy and see what being an uncle was like (she's changing so much... he's missing the three-year-old stage of discovering things). We keep his memories alive with her so she'll know him.

My boy loved the outdoors. Actually, I believe if Seth could have lived outdoors he would have. He loved making forts at a young age and as he grew up was drawn to bonfires. He could sit by a fire for hours. He made a homemade rock fire pit out of large stones he had taken from a nearby creek bed. He was simple, never needing much... just good friends and his family, and of course the love of his life, all made his heart content.

He kept notes in his phone and since his leaving I've been able to read through them. He wrote about his future plans, as well as the toll he believed the accident took on him mentally. At first I wasn't sure what I'd find going through his phone and discovering some of his personal text messages as well as notes he journaled, but we had to know "what was he thinking?!"

Did he leave a "goodbye" note? No. I don't think Seth knew himself at that moment he was consciously making a choice to be gone forever, he just needed a moment, a break away from the battle inside.

The Accident

The day of his accident, Seth was just going from a friend's home to ours; they were traveling the back country road. It was his first time on a side by side.

I remember it like it was yesterday. My husband received the call. Seth's friend thought he died and was frantically asking, "What hospital?" We were in disbelief, they weren't even in the woods yet!!! We jumped in the truck and headed for the hospital, our hearts sinking, just praying, "Dear Lord, please let him be ok."

Seth was confused and with the fear of God in his eyes he asked us, "Am I going to die?" His dad and I both responded, "Absolutely not!" He was scared and could feel how broken he was inside. (Who knew how true that word "broken" would still ring true 22 months later.)

Seth was immediately rushed back into the emergency room, where we learned he had a concussion, shattered teeth, lacerations to his face, and his jaw broken in three locations. Within moments he was transferred to a bigger hospital where doctors and plastic surgeons were awaiting our arrival. We waited for CT (computed

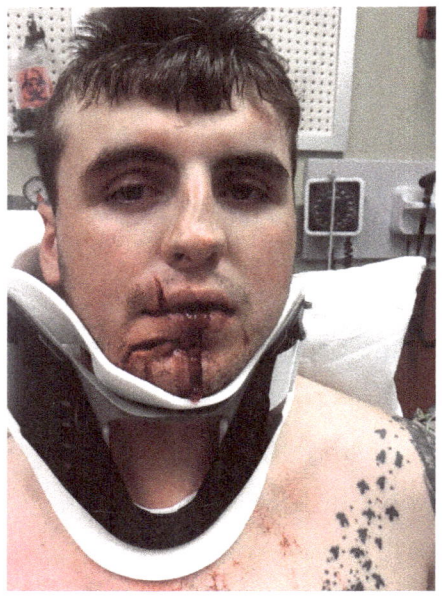
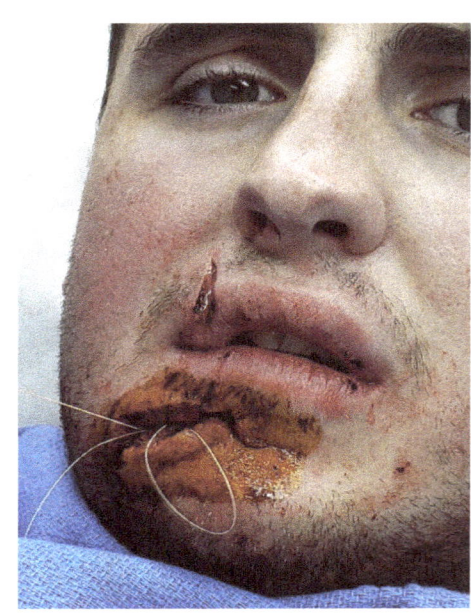

These images are gruesome, but show the severity of the accident. Look at the fear in Seth's eyes.

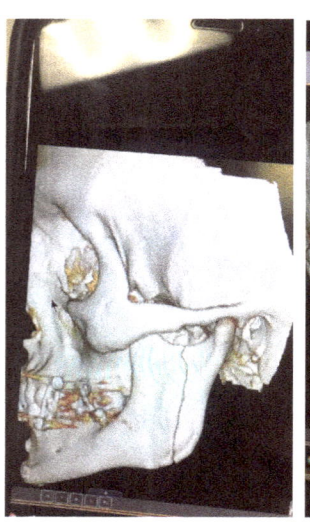
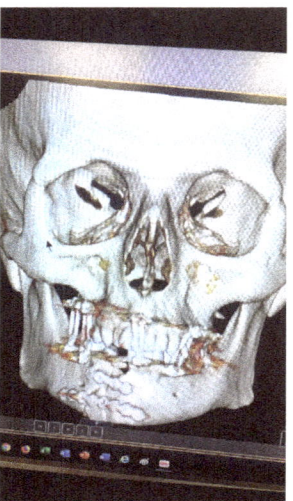
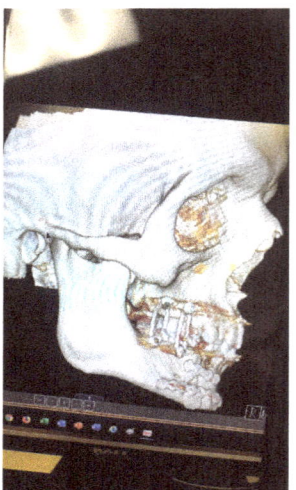

tomography) and MRI (magnetic resonance imaging) scans to be performed. I hit my knees and we prayed. Results came in. "Thank God, no brain damage!!!"

We learned more details and the seriousness of hisinjuries. Seth would need a very intensive surgery consisting of a team of doctors. We're told hematoma and concussion with head trauma, he's going to need surgery for several breaks, but again "no brain damage." He was broken but we felt blessed, we felt we were in the clear… little did we realize we were far from being clear!

Medical terms were spoken, a plan set in motion… we were just thankful he's alive!!

Over the next few days, discussions occur of another hospital that has another set of doctors to perform his nearly six hour surgery. The transfer is made, we arrive at Mercy Medical. Seth is set for surgery. Nervous and scared, we wait and assure him he'll be just fine, he's in good hands. Thank God, all seems to have gone well; although in pain and confusion his mouth was wired shut. We now begin our road of recovery, little did we know recovery would be more than just physical.

We now know the "mental toll" took more havoc over his life than the physical.

What can you do for your loved one? Educate yourself; understand just what the medical terms mean. If you discover something that you feel needs to be addressed, ADVOCATE for them. Voice your concerns.

Ask the questions. You know your loved one better than anyone, don't slip under the radar. I continue to learn more about this topic, even a year later.

Awareness of TBI/PCS has to be part of the Post Op treatment plan for anyone who's suffered injuries as great as Seth did. An injury to the leg or the arm gets a cast and others can sympathize with you. However, injury to the brain, where there's no cast, messes with your psyche and you're left to battle with: "What's wrong with me?"

Don't land in the safety net of medical imaging CT scans and MRIs being negative; they are not detectors of concussion and traumatic brain injury.

Do your research. Learn what scans reveal and what they do not reveal. The information listed below is what I found in the months after Seth was gone. We researched and educated ourselves to understand how one's mind becomes plagued. He is not alone. There are many "walking wounded." What can you do? Educate and advocate.

What to know about CT and MRI scans

Brain scans are usually not helpful for a concussion. A scan can show if there's a fracture or bleeding.

These scans cannot show if you have a concussion

A concussion is different from a fracture or bleeding. A concussion affects how your brain works!!

What MRI & CT Scans Reveal

The CT scan takes pictures to create images of the brain. An MRI creates clear images of brain tissue. They will show bleeding on the brain, a skull fracture, or swelling on the brain.

What MRI & CT Scans Do NOT Reveal

Brain Functioning. Here's why concussions are not "seen" on MRIs or CTs. These scans report back the physical anatomy of the brain – not your brain function. Concussions do not change the appearance of the brain. Concussions change how your brain functions.

Please understand there can be delayed symptoms from a concussion that get worse over time, which will be diagnosed as PCS.

The symptoms that can occur later are

- persistent, low-grade headache
- sleep disturbances
- memory disturbances
- attention disturbances
- concentration
- irritability
- personality changes – easily frustrated, more tearful
- fatigue

(Seth had all the above)

This can all be very detrimental in your "recovery " because here you are, months later, physically feeling better but your mind is starting to glitch and without knowing there's even a condition of PCS or that you could even have delayed symptoms from your concussion you start questioning who you are and your feelings of despair set in. As did for our son.

AmenClinics.com

I happened to find the website of Amen Clinics, which provides so much valuable information to better understand how TBI/Concussion affect the brain and person.

They do something called SPECT IMAGING (single photon emission computed tomography). This type of scan needs to be available to all medical facilities. Time and time again I'm reading CT and MRI are not detectors for brain functioning. CT and MRI scans show if there is any damage to the anatomy or structure of your brain, but these scans cannot tell how your brain is functioning. In fact, after a TBI, CT or MRI scans will often appear normal when there is actually functional damage to the brain that can be detected with SPECT.

I cannot stress enough just how vital this all is.

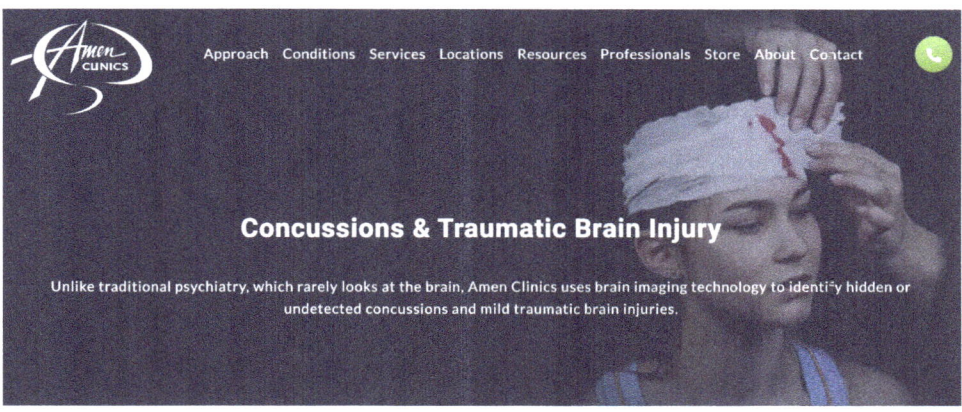

Concussions & Traumatic Brain Injury

Unlike traditional psychiatry, which rarely looks at the brain, Amen Clinics uses brain imaging technology to identify hidden or undetected concussions and mild traumatic brain injuries.

What are Concussions & Traumatic Brain Injuries?

A **concussion** is a type of **traumatic brain injury (TBI)**, which is any disruption in healthy brain functioning due to a bump, blow, blast, or other injury to the head. You don't need to black out or be diagnosed with a concussion to experience lasting cognitive, psychological, or behavioral issues. There are approximately 1.7 million emergency room visits for traumatic brain injury (TBI) in the U.S. annually, and an estimated 300,000 veterans who have sustained TBIs during conflicts. On top of this, there are hundreds of thousands of unreported incidents of head trauma, including undiagnosed concussions each year. Unfortunately for many of those who sustain them, brain injuries that don't result in a loss of consciousness often go unnoticed and are never treated.

Who Gets Head Injuries?

Over 2 million new head injuries occur in the U.S. every year, and the number of concussions is rising, especially among children. From 2010 to 2015, concussion diagnoses jumped 43% among the general population. For young people from 10 to 19 years of age, however, concussion diagnoses skyrocketed 71%. In addition, since 2000, more than 350,000 military veterans have had a Traumatic Brain Injury (TBI).

What are the Core Symptoms?

Research has shown that head injuries are a major cause of mental health problems, but few mental healthcare professionals know it because psychiatry remains the only medical field that rarely looks at the organ it treats. At Amen Clinics, 40% of our patients have experienced a past head injury, and many of them don't remember it.

Head injuries are serious. They can cause a wide range of problems. They can cause confusion, difficulty concentrating, memory problems, moodiness, angry outbursts, balance issues, increased anxiety and even cause you to have suicidal thoughts.

What Causes Head Injuries?

Concussions and brain injuries are caused by a number of reasons. From sports (such as football, baseball, basketball, hockey, soccer, or rugby) to being in an altercation or fight, to falling or even being in a car accident. Believe it or not a simple "fender-bender" can cause significant issues for your brain.

Research shows that concussions & TBI's increase the risk of:

- Depression
- Anxiety and panic disorders
- Drug and alcohol abuse
- ADD/ADHD
- Psychosis
- Post-traumatic stress disorders
- Personality disorders
- Aggression
- Dementia
- Suicide

At the end of the day I know we don't get our son back, but I do know by my speaking out on behalf our family and advocating for our son we may help another family to not have to endure this living hell!!

Unfortunately for us it's all too late, but I'll keep raising our son's voice for he was compassionate about people and doing the right thing so through him maybe he can save you or someone you know and love.

amenclinics.com   Done

What are Concussions & Traumatic Brain Injuries?

A **concussion** is a type of **traumatic brain injury (TBI)**, which is any disruption in healthy brain functioning due to a bump, blow, blast, or other injury to the head. You don't need to black out or be diagnosed with a concussion to experience lasting cognitive, psychological, or behavioral issues. There are approximately 1.7 million emergency room visits for traumatic brain injury (TBI) in the U.S. annually, and an estimated 300,000 veterans who have sustained TBIs during conflicts. On top of this, there are hundreds of thousands of unreported incidents of head trauma, including undiagnosed concussions each year. Unfortunately for many of those who sustain them, brain injuries that don't result in a loss of consciousness often go unnoticed and are never treated.

Could a concussion make a person want to commit suicide?

After Dr. Daniel Amen, Founder and CEO of Amen Clinics, wrote a column on head trauma in a Northern California newspaper, he was contacted by a woman who told him a very sad story. The woman said her daughter had been a model child up until the time she had a bike accident when she was about 18. She hit a branch, flew over the handlebars, landed face-first on the street, and momentarily lost consciousness. Since then, everything changed. The young woman went from being happy and cooperative to angry and moody. Therapy didn't help, and the young woman eventually took her own life when she was just 20 years old. Her mother was heartbroken, especially when she discovered the connection between concussions and suicide and that there are things you can do to help heal the brain after a concussion. If only she had known earlier, she said.

A major factor in his accident

There are factors that could have changed the course in my son's life that day; one may argue the means of travel. However, the only thing that made the side by side different from a car is that it wasn't plated with a license. Had the mailbox not been obstructed by tall weeds and been conformed to being made of a break away post, there would have been a completely different outcome. Instead of a trip to the emergency room, the boys would have made a trip to our local hardware store and an embarrassing walk up to the homeowner's door to replace a mailbox.

Here comes my plea to homeowners to be in compliance with AASHTO (American Association of State Highway and Transportation Officials) guidelines of support post for your mailbox. A plea to ask people to conform to the specifications of USPS boxes – guidelines and specifications; stipulations and to use the proper support post as stated in AASHTO guidelines. The guidelines are established and written in a Guide for Erecting Mailboxes published by AASHTO.

It is the homeowner's responsibility to maintain the area around the mailbox and post it should be clear of weeds and debris.

See pages 78-79 for more details about what you can do to support this.

Healing isn't a straight line. It can feel like you're lost and going backward at times. It often doesn't feel good and can... See More

Seth still had a fight in him, even after everything he'd been through. Just a few months after the accident.

The Aftermath

At first in his recovery, Seth was on top of the mountain. He had made it so far, but then got snatched off the backside. He was encouraging, had hope – realizing how lucky he was to be alive. Seth wasn't about drama so he didn't go into great detail on FB about the accident, but he kept putting it out there to keep your head up when faced with a challenge to know you can rise above, just as he was doing.

The injured brain caught up with him in his final months. He didn't realize he was writing his own story – beginning to end – of what he went through after the accident.

Sharing with me what he'd been thinking about the whole night that he'd been sitting there. November 2019 - his thoughts were still there (hopeful) getting back his strength -- Body was healing; mind good // Body better; mind not great

Not understanding concussion brain, Seth saw a whole new him. He didn't recognize himself, and at least at one point he wrote a note of why he hates himself. It is hard for us as his family to handle this information.

What to look for in your loved one: depression, anger, mood shifts, headaches, insomnia, self doubt, fatigued, insecure with self. Having a hard time enjoying the things you used to. Emotional roller coaster.

He made broken look beautiful.

It's said pictures are worth a thousand words, they really are. It's crazy the story to be seen as we go through photos over the last couple of years. If there was a time I thought we'd lose him it was right after his accident.. not now!! Just looking through pictures immediately you can see the toll it took on his body (the physical) and through his words ~he's his true self he wrote of his accident but The LIGHT was still in him.. he was going to rise above it... now looking at photos he's made a comeback physically but the mind.. it's changed (through his own notes ~ he writes of not feeling the same since his accident... "thinking" it's taken a toll on him to some words that just breaks me to my core... because I know him. This wasn't his true self. He'd never write of "hating himself." It was within the last couple of months of his life that his despair began... the darkness was taking hold...

(We had no idea) … then he's reaching out, he's sinking, we're out to eat for my birthday first words to me he ask me to make a appointment to talk with someone.. (I say of course I tell him he's been through a lot .. I'm happy to know he wants to talk with someone - I share this with my husband, I make the appointment the next day they schedule it 24 days out (that needs to be addressed: 24 days is way too far out for someone who's suffering what we didn't realize and now understanding the seriousness of TBI/PCS, but the professionals should know .. the minute I said my son would like to talk to a therapist he's been through a lot over the last 21 months he was in a accident THAT should have rung a bell... he should have been seen asap and not had to wait!! Waiting cost him more silence, more time to feel lost and that there was something wrong with him; the appointment was made June 29 and scheduled out to July 23 "6" days too late!!! He's gone July 17, 2021!!

I'm numb, I feel blindsided. What just happened… Seth loved life, he loved his fiancé, he loved us… he'd never left us all this way.

I can give a million reasons Seth had to live... I can give zero he'd chose to leave!!

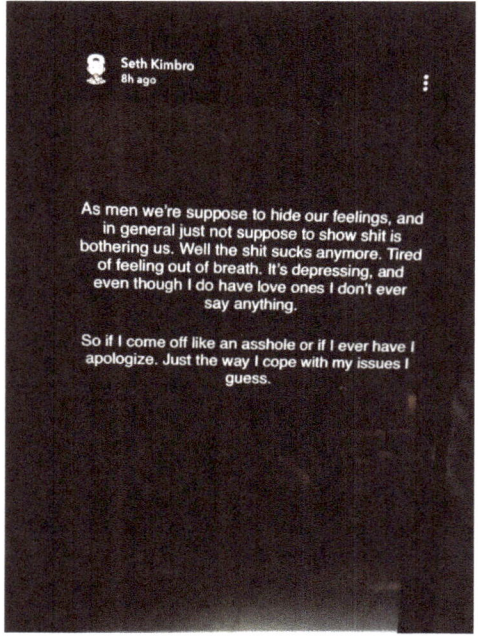

Seth Kimbro
8h ago

As men we're suppose to hide our feelings, and in general just not suppose to show shit is bothering us. Well the shit sucks anymore. Tired of feeling out of breath. It's depressing, and even though I do have love ones I don't ever say anything.

So if I come off like an asshole or if I ever have I apologize. Just the way I cope with my issues I guess.

A post Seth made around May 2021 expressing what he was going through to those who were listening.

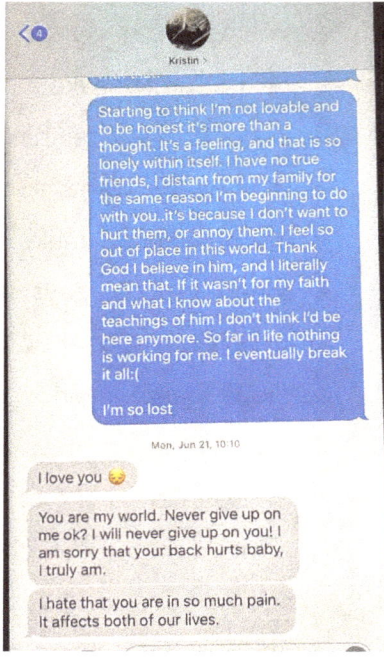

Kristin

Starting to think I'm not lovable and to be honest it's more than a thought. It's a feeling, and that is so lonely within itself. I have no true friends, I distant from my family for the same reason I'm beginning to do with you..it's because I don't want to hurt them, or annoy them. I feel so out of place in this world. Thank God I believe in him, and I literally mean that. If it wasn't for my faith and what I know about the teachings of him I don't think I'd be here anymore. So far in life nothing is working for me. I eventually break it all:(

I'm so lost

Mon, Jun 21, 10:10

I love you 😣

You are my world. Never give up on me ok? I will never give up on you! I am sorry that your back hurts baby, I truly am.

I hate that you are in so much pain. It affects both of our lives.

Less than a month before he was gone.

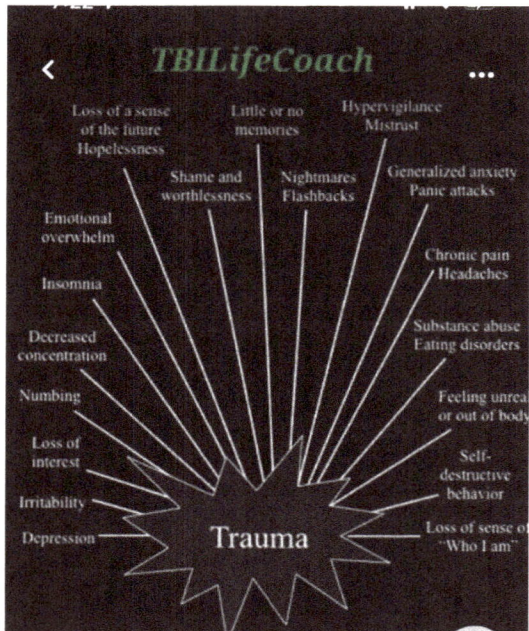

TBILifeCoach

Loss of a sense of the future
Hopelessness

Little or no memories

Hypervigilance
Mistrust

Shame and worthlessness

Nightmares
Flashbacks

Generalized anxiety
Panic attacks

Emotional overwhelm

Chronic pain
Headaches

Insomnia

Decreased concentration

Substance abuse
Eating disorders

Numbing

Feeling unreal or out of body

Loss of interest

Self-destructive behavior

Irritability

Depression

Loss of sense of "Who I am"

Trauma

The Brain Flip

Seemed fine in many ways, he found a great woman who became is fiancé while he grew stronger. They had just Just moved into their apartment. He was just preparing for a new job. He didn't understand (nor did we) the battle he was undergoing.

5/16/21 - He could feel how broken he was physically on the inside. And then over the course of months he's healing… but the brokenness starts all over but this time it's mentally, the mind, his brain it's changing.. he isn't recognizing himself and although "we" see Seth. he begins to lose sight of who he is and the battle within begans. The brain is funny like that ~ it's all scrambled now, making him question his own worth!!

There's havoc, he's reaching out, he's questioning… but he's in "unknown territory."

He hears our words of encouragement, "You look great," but understand "you've been through alot," but look how far you've come… we realize now that was only helping in the moment… The brain fog began, the self doubt stays and takes residence in his head… he wants help, he reaches out… but then he feels fine, but that now only lasts until the next wave pushes him back down… he drifts off further until he feels unseen and he just lets go.

Now I'll share some messages that you can read from his text and notes written by him within the last few months of taking his life… you can just see through his words the self doubt, the loss of hope… his mind has now casted the doubts… he's changing and is uncertain why, physically he's looking great and healing but now mentally the havoc begans…

And here are text /notes that are very hard for me to read… he feels hopeless, the change has taken place…

And it's the "change" that is described in so many artifact's that I find… it's endless how much knowledge there is if only YOU KNOW TO LOOK FOR IT. To know Seth, and us, he'd been all about getting help so much sooner and realizing this wasn't him. It was part of his injury. This is why I say his life was stolen from him.

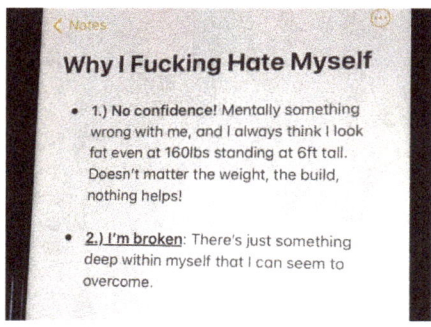

He made a list…

Live for what tomorrow can bring, not for what yesterday has taken away.

Everything's Not Fine

We and Seth learned to live with the aftermath of trauma. It seemed like everything was fine, but it really wasn't. Seth started to experience an internal dilemma. He couldn't understand why he hated himself. There was a disconnect for him. His body was getting fit, and his scars had largely healed, but something still wasn't right.

Was looking for counseling: Seth was recognizing in himself the change, he started sharing of just not feeling the same since his accident and opened up to a close friend of some things that felt off like math skills and speaking of the mental toll he thinks the accident took on him... actually recalling the moment when everything took place he just said "fuck it, I'm fine."

Almost a year late... DON'T SECOND GUESS your feelings or your decision to seek help. It is never too late. Ask others for help we're all in this together

The brain is funny like that - neurotransmitters were short-fusing and wreaking havoc on his mind, causing self doubt and worth. Brain fogs (head hurting all the time).

His math skills were messed up - splitting the cost

of pizza with friends, told me he had a hard time thinking of how to count easy math think of how much he needed to pay. Small math skills were difficult, which was odd for him.

Aggravated with small things that normally wouldn't have gotten to him. Feels distant, self doubt sets in. Shares with fiancé his feelings and the roller coaster he feels on. Late June canoe trip speaks with a friend of feeling off, just recognizes that something is not right - he wasn't feeling like his pre-injury self. Feels his focus and memory has been off. Told his friend in the boat that he didn't feel like himself anymore.

June 2021 reaching out questioning his feelings, self doubt something's not right. Has me make an appointment to speak with a therapist.

July 17, 2021, our world as we've known it stops.

- THE CONCUSSION COMMUNITY

Hill / Seth 💔

September 2021

⚠️ Trigger Warning ⚠️

What suicide looks like and the reality of when you leave this world.

It's taken me over a month to be able to piece this together and write things. When I first started this it said a week, then a month, now it's a month and a half. I add something new every day/couple days when I have thoughts hit me. And I'm sure as time continues to pass us by there will be more I see, learn, and feel. But since today is National Suicide Awareness day I felt I needed to bring myself to finish it.

It's crazy how a month can go by and feel like it was just yesterday but also 100 years ago all at the same time. I know this is the closest I'll be to the last time I physically seen/hugged and spoke to him, and also the longest I've ever went without him.

I've come to a conclusion that the best way I can describe losing a sibling after having them in your life for 24 years the way I have is like walking down the road minding your own business and then all of a sudden you're cut directly in half. The other half of you is just completely gone and your left standing there wondering what just happened, feeling lost, but you still have to walk around with half of you missing and nothing makes sense.

Suicide is a word no one wants to hear. Nobody wants to talk about it, see it, feel it, hear it, believe it or bring it to the surface.

Maybe we think if we don't talk about it or just pretend it's not there that it will go away rather it's in us or a loved one.

But I've seen and heard so much in this last month and a half. Things I've never wanted to see, feel, or hear. But I want to bring a few things to the surface because I can only imagine that when someone is in that dark place they aren't thinking clearly. They aren't seeing everything we are going to see when they're gone. The things I've seen and felt. And maybe if they do, they will reach out and speak about it rather than just to bury and hide it until it consumes them and it's too late and seems like their only option.

I'm here to tell you suicide is NOT your only option.

To the person who ever feels like you no longer want to live, or have the will/ fight to live.

To the person who suffered a traumatic brain injury or any traumatic experience and it's affected you to the point you feel something is wrong with you and it's your only "way out"

The person who feels the world would be a better place without you.

The person who is going through any kind of struggle mentally, physically, financially.

The person having family or relationship issues.

The person who suffers from ptsd.

The mom who suffers from postpartum.

Whatever the case may be, let me tell you, when you're contemplating taking your life and you have the thoughts of "I'm not enough" "life is too hard" "they would be better off without me" whatever the thoughts are that go

through your head (some of us will never know) but what I want you to picture instead of those thoughts are the reality of when you leave this world. These are the things that happen when you leave this world and make

YOUR pain stop (and trust me I don't say it in a judgmental way because I know it has to take so much strength, confusion, and pain to end your life. But you aren't just making your pain stop. Your making your entire heart stop and the minute you do it everyone who loves you, there heart stops too and a piece is ripped out and never to be whole again.

This is what I want you to picture when you have those thoughts.

Picture your sister running in the house at 1am to wake up your parents in a dead sleep to tell them you've done something to yourself as the dogs go crazy and they are half awake trying to understand what your saying while trying to throw clothes on so they can leave the house.

Your Mom signing your death certificate with tears streaming down her face because she signed your birth certificate and never thought she would be doing this one too.

Dad walking in to all the flowers delivered and looking through all of the cards shaking his head in disbelief or whispering when he talks for the next few weeks because he's fighting back tears and has had a lump in his throat from crying for days.

Your friends coming over getting ready to go pack all of your stuff up and move it out of your apartment you were so excited to live in and make a place of your own with your fiancé.

Your little cousin who was waiting for his air soft gear to come in that you recommended to him crying and sleeping in your gear you gave him when he went to sleep the night he found out.

Your fiancé having to have her entire world flipped upside down having to move back home, and have her parents cancel the wedding venue you two booked and un plan her entire future that she had with you being left with nothing but an engagement ring, all the love she had for you, and an empty date for the start of your guys' future.

Your sister having to walk down the aisle next year knowing you aren't standing next to her fiancé when you should be there.

Your 2 year old niece picking up the canvas picture of your face and smiling and kissing it saying your name when we ask her where you are.

Your little sister not wanting to walk away from your casket and tell you bye for the last time, while

She kisses the top of your head.

Your family having to search for signs you left them because it's the only hope they have left of seeing you.

This is the reality of what happens when you leave this earth.

I can promise you the world needs you and is a better place with you in it. I can promise you that someone is willing to help you, talk to you, and listen.

YOuR feelings matter. YOu matter.

There are 8 billion people in the world.

If you're reaching out and feel unheard, reach out somewhere else because there are people who may not even know you and are still rooting for you.

There is hope for you.

Please whatever you're going through and whatever you do, just always be here tomorrow 🦋

#timetotalk #BeHereTomorrow #suicidprevention2021
#1-800-273-8255 national suicide prevention lifeline

TBI Life Coach
Nov 16 · 🌐

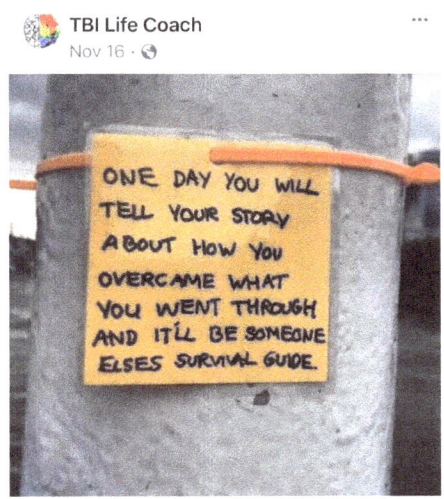

Kathryn Severs BSN, RN Last Updated: July 22, 2022
Cognitive FX
"Family & Friends: How to Help Someone with a Concussion or TBI"

How to Help Someone with Traumatic Brain Injury Recovery
1. Help them break down their tasks
2. Learn their triggers
3. Monitor their overstimulation
4. Make home a friendlier place
5. Help them slowly expand their comfort zone
6. Assume ownership of tasks they can't handle for now
7. Support them during treatment

Understanding Your Loved One's Brain Injury
Myth: The best way to recover from a mild traumatic brain injury is to stay in a dark room and rest.

Fact: An active recovery is better. Patients who try some physical activity (to the extent that they can) and do cognitive exercises in addition to resting recover better and faster.

Myth: Symptoms of a concussion go away after two weeks.

Fact: While most mild TBI patients recover within two weeks, some take longer. Up to 30% of people who sustain a concussion have symptoms that linger for months or years after their injury (a condition known as post-concussion syndrome). This happens when the patient's neurons don't communicate efficiently with the blood vessels that supply them with energy, a process called neurovascular coupling.

Myth: You have to experience loss of consciousness to get a mild traumatic brain injury.

Fact: Concussions can come from a blow to the head, whiplash, or jostling of the brain. You don't have to lose consciousness. Concussion-like illness can also come from other circumstances, such as carbon monoxide poisoning, bacterial and viral disease, chemotherapy, mini-strokes, and more.

Myth: Severe traumatic brain injury symptoms will never get better after initial rehab.

Fact: We believe recovery is life long. Why? Because we've seen it. And because the brain's neuroplasticity allows it to keep adjusting to your injury. While their brain may never make a full recovery, they can keep making progress, even if they've sustained some irreparable brain damage.

https://www.cognitivefxusa.com/blog/how-to-help-someone-with-traumatic-brain-injury-concussion

The Model Systems Knowledge Translation Center (MSKTC) is a national center operated by the American Institutes for Research® (AIR®) that translates health information into easy to understand language and formats for patients with spinal cord injury, traumatic brain injury, and burn injury and their families and caregivers.

https://msktc.org/tbi/factsheets/depression-after-traumatic-brain-injury

Depression After Traumatic Brain Injury

What is depression?

Depression is a feeling of sadness, loss, despair or hopelessness that does not get better over time and is overwhelming enough to interfere with daily life. There is cause for concern when feeling depressed or losing interest in usual activities occurs at least several days per week and lasts for more than two weeks.

Symptoms of depression include:

- Feeling down, sad, blue or hopeless.
- Loss of interest or pleasure in usual activities.
- Feeling worthless, guilty, or that you are a failure.
- Changes in sleep or appetite.
- Difficulty concentrating.
- Withdrawing from others.
- Tiredness or lack of energy.
- Moving or speaking more slowly, or feeling restless or fidgety.
- Thoughts of death or suicide.

Feeling sad is a normal response to the losses and changes a person faces after TBI. However, prolonged feelings of sadness or not enjoying the things you used to enjoy are often key signs of depression, especially if you also have some of the other symptoms listed above.

How common is depression after TBI?

Depression is a common problem after TBI. About half of all people with TBI are affected by depression within the first year after injury. Even more (nearly two-thirds) are affected within seven years after injury. In the general population, the rate of depression is much lower, affecting fewer than one person in 10 over a one-year period. More than half of the people with TBI who are depressed also have significant anxiety.

What causes depression after TBI?

Many different factors contribute to depression after TBI, and these vary a great deal from person to person.

- **Physical changes in the brain due to injury.** Depression may result from injury to the areas of the brain that control emotions. Changes in the levels of certain natural chemicals in the brain, called neurotransmitters, can cause depression.
- **Emotional response to injury.** Depression can also arise as a person struggles to adjust to temporary or lasting disability, losses or role changes within the family and society.
- **Factors unrelated to injury.** Some people have a higher risk for depression due to inherited genes, personal or family history, and other influences that were present before the brain injury.

 **NEWS**

Home / News / Healthiest Communities / TBI Deaths in the U.S.

Suicide Is Top Cause of Deaths Tied to Traumatic Brain Injury

Suicides surpassed car crashes as the top cause of TBI-related deaths in recent years, a new study shows.

By Gaby Galvin   Nov. 21, 2019

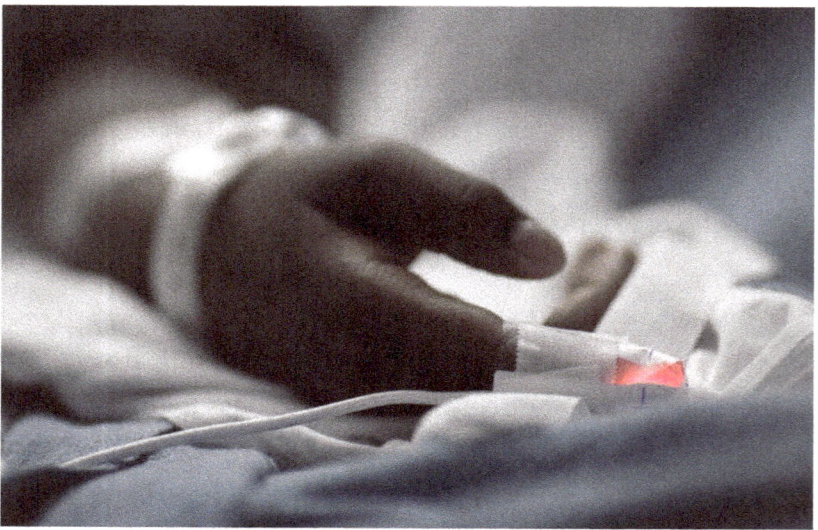

From 2014 to 2017, the traumatic brain injury-linked death rate rose from 16.3 to 17.5 per 100,000 people. (GETTY IMAGES)

Deaths tied to traumatic brain injuries have risen amid higher rates of suicides and accidental falls in the U.S., a new analysis says.

Every year, millions of people are hospitalized or go to the ER for traumatic brain injuries, which are usually caused by violent blows to the head and can lead to death or disability. There were 61,131 TBI-linked deaths in 2017 alone, and nearly half of these deaths were by suicide or homicide from 2015 to 2017, according to the study released Thursday by the Centers for Disease Control and Prevention.

https://www.usnews.com/news/healthiest-communities/articles/2019-11-21/suicide-is-top-cause-of-deaths-tied-to-traumatic-brain-injury

Post Concussion Syndrome Depression

A SISTER'S REQUEST

What it looks like: I'm fine, I've been through a lot, doctors said I have no brain damage, but why do I now struggle and it just seems to be getting worse with time? In the beginning of his accident, Seth had a strive for life. He wrote of overcoming all he'd been through and encouraging others that you can overcome tragedy with perseverance and family. Seth spoke of his obstacles, but had goals and plans to make it up the mountain before him. Then over the course of time it's as if the lights began to dim. He lost his will even though he had so much in his favor now.

Important to know just because there's no brain damage doesn't mean there's no brain injury (MRI/CT scans don't pick up brain injury) ~ knowledge is key.

What actually happened to Seth Kimbo? I feel with March being Traumatic Brain Injury Awareness month I would like to speak out on my brother's behalf and give an insight to the "why" that many of you have been questioning for months now. In just four months it will be a year that he's been gone and he still deserves to be heard and not misunderstood. Seth wasn't some depressed guy who hated life and had nothing. He didn't grow up battling depression. He was the exact opposite. He had a very close family, an absolutely beautiful, fun, sweet, loving fiancé, and the best and craziest of friends, from the time he was little to 24 years old. He was excited to be starting a new job, he had just moved into his first apartment and was loving it, had just spent weeks picking out house items and furniture, and, very proud of his findings and what he had put together, had just booked and planning a wedding, was excited to be in my wedding, had pets that he adored, a niece he was crazy about, a mom (who he wanted to open a little restaurant with one day) and dad (who he loved riding motorcycles with), and he loved them all very much. Two sisters he loved and wanted to always be around to protect. He LOVED life. Anyone who knows him, knows he loved life and lived it to the fullest. He loved making people happy, making people laugh, standing up for others and what he believed. He was strong, extremely intelligent, passionate about what and who he loved, and he had life plans and goals. He was making future plans and excited the very week of his life ending, actually. My brother didn't want to end his life. He wanted to end the fight in his head that he didn't understand after his accident. He wanted to end the "new life as he knew it." He wanted to end the constant battle in his head that had taken over that he didn't understand. The "you look fine and healed on the outside, so what's wrong with you?" That he had to ask himself every day. He wanted to end the chronic pain that was irritating and slowed him down from his pre-accident self, the missing teeth that no one else really noticed, but he had to feel and look in the mirror and hate every single day. The irritation and aggravation that was trying to take over. He never wanted to end his life and not be here for his family, future fiancé, friends, and future plans. He wanted to end this new version of him that he didn't understand and was tired of battling against everyday. So, if you or someone you know has been in an accident and suffered a mild or traumatic brain injury, and you "recover" on the outside but don't feel right even after your wounds are healed and time has passed, don't be afraid to talk to someone!

Trust your instincts that something isn't right. You know yourself better than anyone else. Just because you look fine and "better" on the outside, doesn't mean you're healed on the inside. And that is okay. It can be. There is help, and therapy and people who will understand what you're going through. You're not crazy and you're not alone. It's not just in your head, it's made an impact on your brain, literally. And you don't have to face the depression, confusion, pain, fatigue, or aggravation alone until you can't take it anymore and give up your life.

Seth will always be his true self to all of us who loved him no matter how he was feeling on the inside that we couldn't see. And although we would love to have him healed and here with us on earth, he is no longer battling anymore. Do him and our family a favor and if you or anyone you know is going through this please reach out before it's too late.

A MOTHER'S SEARCH

I would wake through the night with such grief and just wishing it had been me and that his life could have been spared. I made it my mission to learn and understand every aspect to how exactly depression and the correlation of suicide, trauma, PCS all tied together. I stopped at nothing, I spent hours upon hours online, researching, looking for vital information about why our son wasn't here. 11/28/21 was the day I discovered an article* and it all clicked together for me. I began to write to his doctors. I thought, *Wow, I've discovered something they all need to know and understand... I will share my writings.*

The article in *The Washington Post* stated a correlation between suicide and mild concussion: "They found a suicide rate of 31 deaths per 100,000 patients -- three times the population norm. The mean time between a mild concussion and suicide was 5.7 years, and each additional concussion raised suicide risk."

* https://www.washingtonpost.com/news/to-your-health/wp/2016/02/22/the-terrifying-link-between-concussions-and-suicide/

I actually spoke to his primary physician and surgeon a week after Seth passed, just trying to piece everything together. Having both Doctors tell me that they, "didn't see this coming!!" to now fast forward five months and a lot of our own research... my question to them was, "Really??" I felt angered. "How could you miss it?!"

It almost seems inevitable with a head trauma such as Seth endured!! So then the real question is... why weren't we informed after Seth's accident about the severity of the depression side of a TBI/PCS?!

I get it, no one wants to have fingers pointed at them and, no, it didn't start from the doctors. The root cause is the structure of a mailbox also known as a DFO (deadly fixed object) that was made of unforgiving material!

However I do wish there had been knowledge given to our family, our son of TBI/PCS DEPRESSION. This should have been listed as part of his Post Op injury care!!

We shouldn't have felt as if we had discovered "the light bulb" from simply Googling depression / suicide after an accident~ EVERTHING we needed to know. Right there in black and white!!! My daughter and I sat for hours on end just reading and researching everything from PTSD to PCS, there was so much correlation of head injury and suicide. So still thinking we've put this all together... "it all makes sense now"... I eagerly contacted his surgeon through text (who told me "he was shocked" and "didn't see this coming") and re replied I could reach out to him anytime and expressed his sincere apologies for the loss of our son.

I sent him my findings, only to get no response. I thought he'd be just as ecstatic to learn what we are finding out. After much silence in the days to follow, I realized... he knows. I'm sure his heart sank. He cared for Seth not just as his patient but he had a connection with him ~ you could see it when we went to our follow up appointments ~ he always greeted Seth with "Seth, my man," and a fist bump, to even having the same tattoo in common. He'd compliment him on his progress, even once telling him him he was going to be a "lady slayer." We looked forward to these visits. He was just very encouraging to Seth. He's a good doctor, as is his medical physician. I don't feel they intentionally withheld vital information or intended Seth harm, I've read enough to know this depression side of a concussion can be tricky.

It is known as the "walking wounded," "a silent killer," and even to its victim it plays havoc as it did to Seth, ultimately costing him his own sanity and life. My God, he was just 24 with a whole life ahead of him, there is such an emptiness without him in our lives. Seth had dreams, he had a beautiful future ahead for himself. He had made it through this storm, he was on the upside to all he had been through. God, why?!?!?!

The best thing I can do for Seth now is be his voice. To help others to know and even doctors! OPEN THE

DOOR TO YOUR PATIENTS' MINDS... even if they appear well. Start the conversation. Give them an opportunity to share if they sometimes feel any of the following and try to get them to talk in detail of what that looks like to them:

depressed - mood swings - helplessness
hopeless - anger - exhausted - worthless
a roller coaster of emotions and you
just aren't feeling like pre-injury you

*** You're not alone or to blame. *** Your feelings are real, but they ARE a side effect of your accident. TBI/PCS depression is something we can treat, we can work through...

Give your loved ones hope again, let them know they're not going crazy!!! It's not just in their head. Help them to swim, not sink!!! This would open the door for them to actually reach out for help and it would help their families and loved ones to help them through this darkness, through this side of injury. TBI/PCS depression is very real!!!! Knowledge is key ~ to ALL involved!!! Patients, families, and our healthcare providers!!!!

God bless the knowledge that's out there This Needs To Be Known, There Needs To Be More Awareness for Everyone. Signs should be posted throughout the medical office / facilities ~ all this should not have cost Seth his life!!! God bless our lives and loved ones help us to forgive those who have failed us and who failed Seth!!!!!!

I journaled all this within the first five months of Seth being gone... for I realized ~ I had not discovered this silent killer... It is known yet unknown that needs to change and so I began to advocate for Seth and raise his voice. This is why I write, lives can be changed, victims of concussion don't have to suffer and a concussion can wreak havoc on all walks of life... No one is immuned.

Suicide is the third leading cause of death for Seth's age range. Overall, some 40,000 people die annually by suicide in the United States. That may not seem like a big number, but it is huge. That's 40,000 families that are affected by this tragedy. I don't know if others truly dig into know and realize why suicide has taken their loved ones. My family wanted answers, so we dug. Of course not all suicides are PCS depression, but a vast majority are and I can share of just a few individuals, like my son, who have died and they all have something in common other than suicide... a accident, a jolt, a hit, a shaken head, face , or skull... a concussion or TBI... that speaks volumes in my world now!!

I found this video on Seth's phone. I was stunned to see the date July 15... just two days before the moment that changed our whole lives. His freedom is there. He was having a good moment. His mind wasn't taking control over him. He was feeling his soul. He bobs and dances in the video.

WHEN YOU ARE HEALTHY

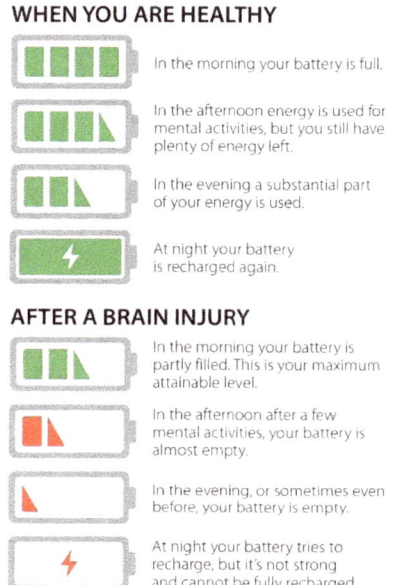

In the morning your battery is full.

In the afternoon energy is used for mental activities, but you still have plenty of energy left.

In the evening a substantial part of your energy is used.

At night your battery is recharged again.

AFTER A BRAIN INJURY

In the morning your battery is partly filled. This is your maximum attainable level.

In the afternoon after a few mental activities, your battery is almost empty.

In the evening, or sometimes even before, your battery is empty.

At night your battery tries to recharge, but it's not strong and cannot be fully recharged.

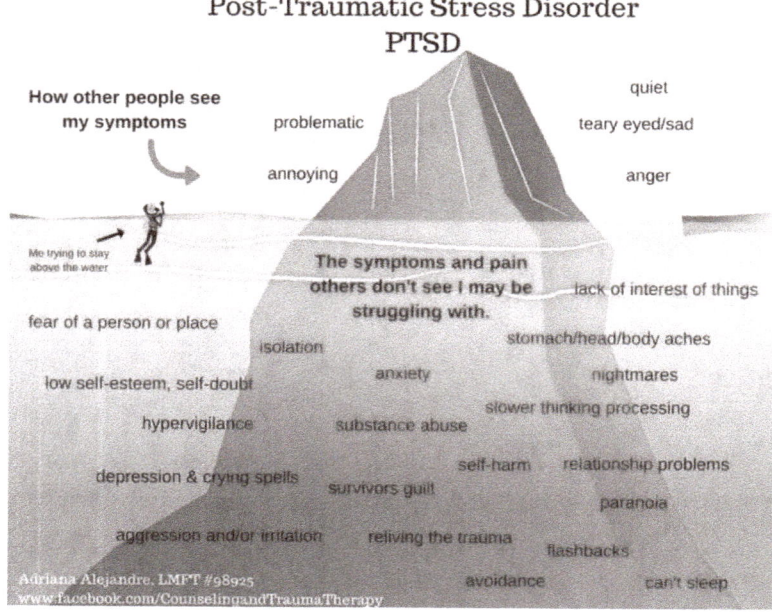

What Can YOU Do?

What we've done in a year of your absence... we grieve you, we miss you, we searched for you, and now we have raised your voice!!! Knowing you, there had to be more! You were so full of life, it wasn't like you to just walk away forever.

This brings us to our present day. We now raise your voice, Seth Michael, by advocating for you and bringing awareness to all counts...

We advocate for our son and bring light to this darkness – both the medical side *and* the guidelines of building and constructing a mailbox and it's proper support.

Within five months of your absence we began sending out the knowledge of TBI and PCS depression. The doctor's office has put them in rooms for patients to see and relate, just in case they're in a unknown space in their own life.

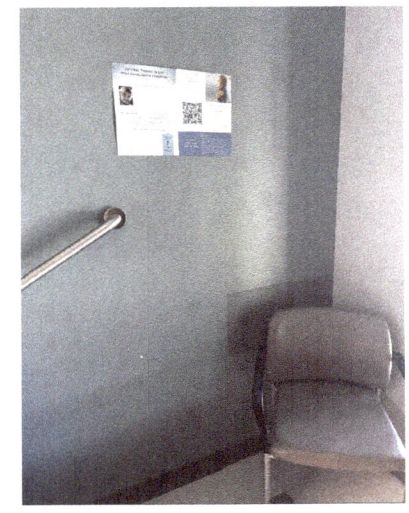

The flyer we created (in full on next page) hangs in Seth's doctor's office to bring awareness.

This is the poster we made with support from Cognitive Fx.

SUICIDAL THOUGHTS AND POST-CONCUSSION SYNDROME

What can you do?

A LETTER FROM A MOTHER

I've spent the last 174 days just trying to piece this all together. 174 days since We've heard your voice, seen you, hugged you.

So, I will try my best to shed some light on the darkness that Seth faced that night. Seth was suffering from a traumatic brain injury and post-concussion syndrome depression. It is a silent killer. It's an inner battle many suffer after a traumatic injury. Although Seth miraculously lived through the accident, his injuries were much more than a broken jaw in 3 places, and shattered chin & missing teeth... he was living with a much deeper wound.

The battle of TBI/post-concussion syndrome, the depression side of his accident.

At the time we felt so blessed that Seth survived the accident, doctors had said it was a miracle!! Little did he or we realize the effects the TBI/ Concussion would plague in his mind over the next 22 months. I guess you could say "Seth made Broken look Beautiful" so, as his family we vow to our son to bring more awareness to such a debilitating illness.

Seth had dreams, he had a beautiful life to live! I'd like to talk so Seth can be heard & he's not just the boy "who took his life" He had so much to look forward too. Seth loved life, he would have chosen to live! Maybe someone you know, or love has been in a Traumatic accident, or has had a Concussion. Know the signs, reach out talk to them, let them know it's real, that it's not just in their head!

Just because there's no brain damage, doesn't mean there's no brain injury.

- Laura Kimbro.
Family of Seth Kimbro (1997-2021)

GET HELP NOW

- Call 911 or your local emergency number now
- Call a suicide hotline
- Make your environment safe

- Don't keep suicidal thoughts to yourself
- Know that people **do** get through this

WHY DO I FEEL SUICIDAL AFTER A BRAIN INJURY?

Suicidal thoughts can due to an **emotional response** to the brain injury and may also be caused by **physical changes** in the brain.

A brain injury can be **emotionally traumatic**. Difficulties often arise as patients struggle to adjust to their new reality, even if the concussion symptoms are just temporary. Patients often feel helplessness and hopelessness and being told that their issues are "all in your head" by friends or doctors can further compound these emotions. To make things worse, issues such as losing a job or a change in family dynamics can create feelings of hopelessness, irritability, and frustration. Some patients react with mood swings, outbursts of anger or they may become sad and withdrawn. As these patients realize they're unable to return to their pre-injury lifestyle, the added stress of coping with symptoms such as headaches, dizziness, and cognitive issues put patients at increased risk for suicidal thoughts.

Suicidal thoughts may also result from a **direct impact on the areas of the brain** that control emotions, memory, and executive skills. Studies have shown that concussion patients who go on to develop depression and suicidal thoughts are much more likely to experience damage to the hippocampus and the orbitofrontal cortex.

Studies show that having suicidal thoughts is

7

TIMES

more common in PCS patients than in the general population

HOW TO COPE

WITH SUICIDAL THOUGHTS FROM A BRAIN INJURY

WHAT TO DO

- Talk with someone every day
- Create a schedule
- Make a safety plan
- Exercise
- Find a safe place

WHAT TO AVOID

- Being alone
- Alcohol & Drugs
- Doing things that make you feel worse
- Worrying about your suicidal thoughts

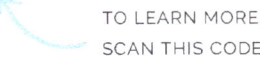

TO LEARN MORE,
SCAN THIS CODE

FAMILY AND FRIENDS

WHAT THEY CAN DO TO HELP

For some, recovering from a head trauma can be overwhelming, while others may see it in a more positive way. Everyone is different, and there is no "normal" recovery journey. However, whether your loved one is feeling apprehensive or a little more upbeat, it's crucial you support them during this period. This can be anything from helping with shopping trips to being a patient listener. Learn to adapt to what they can do. A concussion doesn't mean they stop enjoying activities you did together, but you may just have to do things differently for a while.

Above all, if they open up to you, don't brush off their feelings or ignore what they're saying. This is particularly important if you've noticed any behavior or personality changes that may indicate they're having suicidal thoughts. This could include, for example, having dramatic mood swings or engaging in reckless and impulsive behavior.

YOU ARE NOT ALONE

Even if you've been fighting with suicidal thoughts for a long time, you are not alone.

Data from the Substance Abuse and Mental Health Services Administration (SAMHSA) for 2019 showed that 12 million Americans seriously thought about suicide, and 3.5 million even had a plan. Most people who have suicidal thoughts do not actually act on these feelings and never attempt suicide, but nevertheless, these should never be ignored. Many people before you have gone through the same difficulties and were able to recover and improve their quality of life.

Remember, suicide is an irreversible solution to a temporary problem. It may be difficult to see it at the moment, but the feelings you have now are short lived. With the right medical attention, you won't always feel like this.

Planning a movement in Seth's name

My plan is to make a movement in our son's name to bring more awareness to what *is* and *is not* acceptable regarding the structure and build of mailboxes and posts. Regulations are out there and should be followed. The following organizations share the rules/guidelines on their websites:

- USPS
- FEDERAL HIGHWAY ADMINISTRATION
- IDOT
- AASHTO

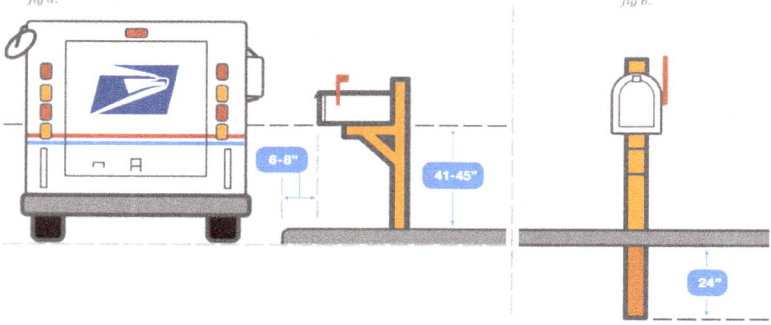

USPS Mailbox Installation Specification:

<u>Height</u>: Vertical height of 41-45 inches from road surface

<u>Mounting</u>: Attachment to the top of the post with a metal bracket that is bolted horizontally through the post. (AASHTO)

<u>Post</u>: Supports should be made of lightweight materials that will easily break away. If metal pipes are used, the pipe should not have a diameter greater than two inches. Wood posts should not be greater than four inches square, or have a diameter of more than four and one-half inches. The post should not be more than 24 inches into the ground and should not be set in concrete. By following these guidelines, the mailbox post will either break or be moved rather than be a safety hazard for motorists and residents. (AASHTO)

<u>Turnout</u>: Minimum 8' wide paved or graveled area from the edge of the traffic way. (USPS, AASHTO, ODOT)

"Awareness is key" and there are guidelines to mailbox and post. It is all public information.

What it SHOULD look like.   What Seth experienced.

Unapproved Structures

Large structures such as I-beam, hand pumps, farm implements or stone/brick structures to support a mailbox along the roadway pose a safety risk to the traveling public and are not permitted.

Caring for humanity

We're all in this together. Will you make this change with me? You can't change what you don't know... but when you do know and you won't change, that breaks my heart. Our son paid the ultimate price for a change that is so very simple to make. **A wooden post is less than $30, our son's life was priceless!!!**

Polar Plunge

We did a Polar Plunge for a chance to be nominated to bring awareness to a good cause. This one is pretty cool because it was something Seth had done every year right outside our own back yard... We created a polar plunge just for you "no cause~just cause"!!

Guys!!!! THIS HAS Seth Kimbro NAME ALLL OVER IT!!!
    SAVE THE DATE: Saturday JANUARY 8,
        10:00 a.m
25.00 entry ~all ENTRIES get a chance to be picked for a Charity of choice~ we'd like to choose "TBI/Post Concussion syndrome Depression" AWARENESS FOR SETH ~,Together WE can be a very Strong Voice for him through this Great Freezing Fund!!! And you best believe he's looking down on all of us with his great big smile and that chuckling laugh of his rooting us on while we take the PLUNGE!!!

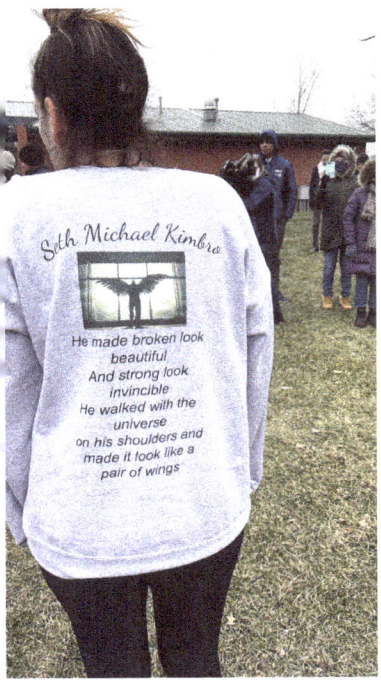

Polar Plunge 2022

Seth Kimbro & his crazy personality did his own polar plunge every year so this was a great way to honor him 💚
#hisfightisourfight
#tbiawareness
#BeHereTomorrow
... See More

Flyers, Groups, Awareness

I've shared some of your information on a couple concussion groups on social media. I've had a few people reach out wondering if this might be what's happening to them, because they can relate to your feelings. I've met some really phenomenal people on this concussion journey and made connections that help me to start writing this book with the hope of "bringing light to the darkness." Seth, You deserve to be heard and not misunderstood.

MENTAL HEALTH AWARENESS MONTH

SUICIDAL THOUGHTS AND
POST-CONCUSSION SYNDROME

Suicidal thoughts can be caused due to an emotional response to the brain injury
and may also be caused by physical changes in the brain.

Patients often feel helplessness and hopelessness, and being told that their issues are
"all in your head" by friends and doctors can further compound these emotions.

You are NOT alone.

Data from the Substance Abuse and Mental Health Services Administration
for 2019 showed that 12 million Americans seriously thought about suicide,
and 3.5 million even had a plan.

Most people who have suicidal thoughts do not actually act on these feelings and never attempt
suicide, but nevertheless, these thoughts should never be ignored. Many people before you have
gone through the same difficulties and were able to recover and improve their quality of life.

IF you are
suicidal or experiencing
severe depression from
Post-Concussion Syndrome
or another cause:

Every time you ship Express
through us in the month of May,

we will donate $5 to:

The Seth Kimbro Memorial Fund

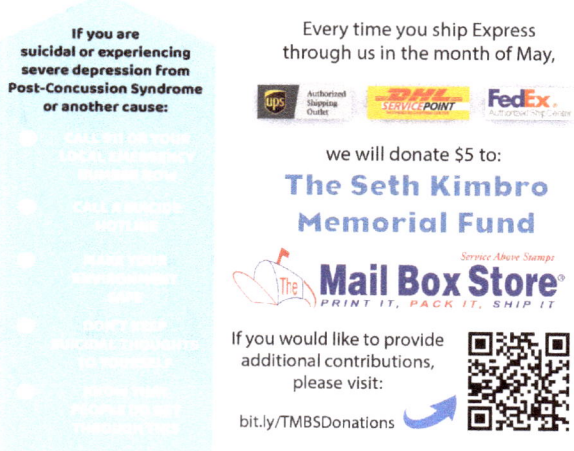

The Mail Box Store
PRINT IT, PACK IT, SHIP IT

If you would like to provide
additional contributions,
please visit:

bit.ly/TMBSDonations

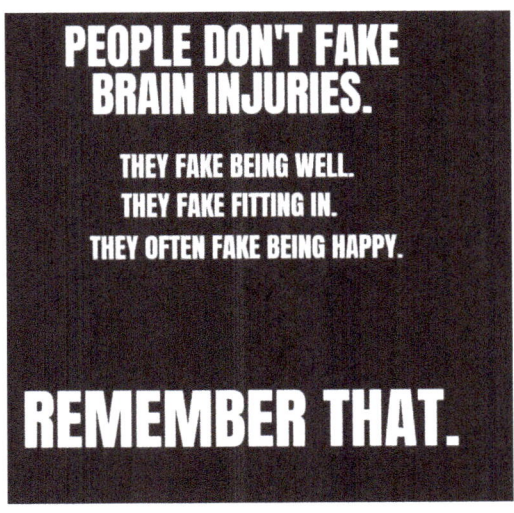

September 2022 we created a billboard to raise awareness in our community.

Battle for Kimbro

We even took to the field for you with the help of some of your great brotherhood of friends and had an air-soft event in your name: *Battle for Kimbro*. The turnout was great and even inspired some of the younger generation to get hooked on the game ~ leaving a path to what you loved and had started, carrying out to what you had promised and planned on: "showing them how to play." In the days after your leaving a few of the young ones you had inspired where, well, "shell shocked" and would say, "but he promised me he'd teach me and play airsoft with me." (Blake and Landon just to name a few.) Seth liked to take these guys under his wing, but telling them the first rule is, "Ya gotta let me shoot you." He'd say, "It's the only way you'll know and it's going to hurt."

Your cousin even lay at night in the days to follow with your gear upon his chest as he laid in confusion... you were building a airsoft gun together!! Where are you?? We scrambled for answers to give. The land owner wants to do an annual awareness event around Seth's birthday.

Family

Battle for Kimbro 2022

We love you Seth michael!!!

TAKING A MOMENT OF SILENCE FOR SETH!!

You played well son!!

Personal Expression

And now we know and now we share all the knowledge we have!! We know you didn't want to leave your life, you just wanted the battle inside to stop.

At Seth's birthday celebration this year, Lexi unveiled her new tattoo – a phrase in Seth's handwriting – from Seth's personal notebook. "Be here tomorrow"

Friendship

One really cool thing we've done with the help of your friends and their families ~ we share your name and have a moment for you. Your name has been written across many hearts. Florida, Colorado, Europe, Mexico, and on the banks of the river. Even at an African sunset.

Seth our strong light... you are so very loved.

Florida
Africa
Mexico
Colorado
💛

Survivors

Survivors of TBI are also struggling. Please read these two messages from two amazing women I have met along my journey of discovery.

Anessa Arehart

TBIs silently affect every aspect of a person's existance.

Mechanical disfunctions such as memory loss, vestibular problems, and headaches are commonly addressed, but on a deeper level lies crushing amounts grief, anger, and mourning for the person that once was.

True healing can only begin when the depth of these emotional traumas piggybacking TBI are addressed with as much importance as their counterparts.

A survivor must be brave and examine both kinds of loss in order to rebuild a happy life.

You don't have to make friends with your trauma, but you must tend to it like a garden.

I go there mentally every day to check-in. I don't stay and wallow, but I do allow myself to recognize the nothingness where my journey began and how my life has blossomed once again over the years.

I already cried about it this morning for a minute.
It never totally goes away... at least it hasn't yet.

But if you work the garden of your mind, it will allow you to embrace, examine, and work though your own experience. No matter how horrible it was, you will eventually soften the edges of heartache and find hope again.

I wrote a book in hopes of helping people like Seth that are teetering on the edge. I was there. I barely pulled myself back from the brink. I could easily have been Seth.

I recognize the depth of your struggles. The author of this book, Laura Kimbro, does too. We both believe that you can survive TBI if you know where to begin and know that you aren't alone. Life can go on. You can be happy again.

Reading successful transformational journeys and finding emotional support are good places to begin. Laura and I have both shared our stories in honor of the folks like Seth who need a little help finding their way out of the darkness. We both hope to lead you back in to the lightness of being.

https://www.anessaarehart.com/
@littlewinghollow

Perri Runion

First things first, I am so so sorry for your loss. This truly breaks my heart to read this about your son, I can only imagine how heartbreaking this experience has been for you. THIS right here is why I have chosen to share my story, so I appreciate you reaching out and sharing yours. I am certain TBI/ PCS is one of the most undiagnosed/misunderstood killers, the culprit behind many health conditions (mental and physcial) and suicide. And yet, so many don't even know there is a correlation - and this includes doctors. Ugh!!

I am so glad that you were able to dig deeper as a family and understand what your son was dealing with, I have no doubt from what you have shared that it is the WHY. Thank you for choosing as a family to raise up his voice and educate those around you. Getting this knowledge out to the world will indeed save lives, I deeply feel that.

And lastly, thank you for reaching out and for encouraging me to speak more!! This has been a wild journey to articulate and I often doubt if sharing will make any difference. But, it's messages like yours that keep me motivated and remind me that it's worth the effort to share. In fact, I have been a little silent lately and this just sparked up my motivation to get back to it. So thank you!

Sending deep love your way for the loss of your son, know that he is looking down at you and your family proud - knowing he is now understood.

Keep fighting the good fight and sharing, together we can save lives!!

IG @perrirunion
FB @theperrirunion

Research

One discovery led to the next...
Here are some clips of what I found on my relentless
search for answers and understanding.

A traumatic brain injury **interferes with the way the brain normally works**. When nerve cells in the brain are damaged, they can no longer send information to each other in the normal way. This causes changes in the person's behavior and abilities.

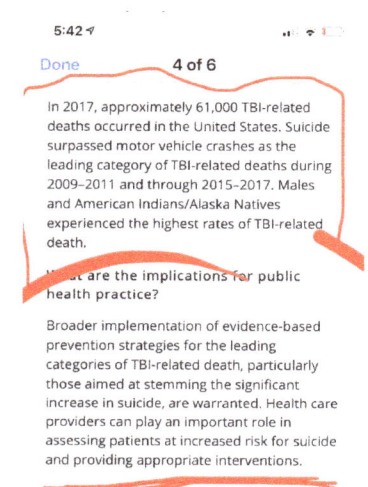

https://msktc.org › tbi › factsheets

Understanding TBI: Part 2 - Brain injury impact on individuals ...

In summary, we have found **increased rates of suicide among patients** with relatively severe traumatic brain injury. Present evidence suggests that no small degree of this increase may be due to premorbid psychosocial factors, as the increase is also present in patients with concussion and cranial fractures.

BMJ https://jnnp.bmj.com › content ⋮

Suicide after traumatic brain injury: a population study

Traumatic brain injury ⋮

Also called: craniocerebral trauma

[Overview] Symptoms Treatments Sp‹

Brain dysfunction caused by an outside force, usually a violent blow to the head.

Traumatic brain injury often occurs as a result of a severe sports injury or car accident.

In 2017, approximately 61,000 TBI-related deaths occurred in the United States. Suicide surpassed motor vehicle crashes as the leading category of TBI-related deaths during 2009–2011 and through 2015–2017. Males and American Indians/Alaska Natives experienced the highest rates of TBI-related death.

What are the implications for public health practice?

Broader implementation of evidence-based prevention strategies for the leading categories of TBI-related death, particularly those aimed at stemming the significant increase in suicide, are warranted. Health care providers can play an important role in assessing patients at increased risk for suicide and providing appropriate interventions.

If You Don't Understand Brain Injuries READ THIS!

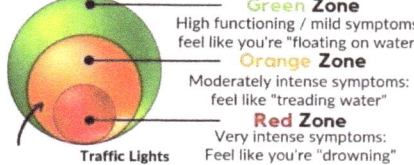

Green Zone
High functioning / mild symptoms:
feel like you're "floating on water"
Orange Zone
Moderately intense symptoms:
feel like "treading water"
Red Zone
Very intense symptoms:
Traffic Lights   Feel like you're "drowning"

A brain injury **is an ILLNESS: Some days...**
- You can **work long hours** and do all the chores (green zone), other days you **struggle to have a shower** (red zone)
- You can **fake a smile and attend social events** (green and orange zone), other days you have to **hide in your room**, recharge, and wait for the storm to pass (red zone)
- ⚠ Please understand this and **don't make someone have to prove how unwell they are** - they're fighting an invisible illness that is life threatening.

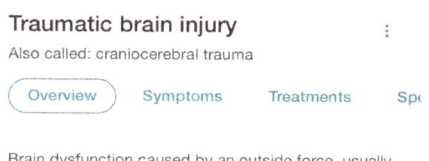

CDC HEADS UP
SAFE BRAIN. STRONGER FUTURE.

News and Announcements

- CDC Reports:
  - ED Visits for Bicycle-related TBIs/Concussions Drop by Half among Children
  - CDC Study Compares Head Impacts in Youth Tackle and Flag Football
  - Deaths from fall-related TBIs are on the rise
  - Suicide is now the leading category of TBI-related deaths
- CDC Programs:
  - HEADS UP to Healthcare Providers online training is now available on CDC Train
  - HEADS UP to School Professionals online training is now available on CDC Train

---

.ıl AT&T 🤶   6:08 AM   🔒 cdc.gov

Symptoms may be difficult to sort out as they are similar to other health problems

After a mild TBI or concussion:

- A person may not recognize or admit that they are having problems
- A person may not understard how the symptoms they are experiencing affect their daily activities
- Problems may be overlooked by the person with the mild TBI or concussion, family members, or healthcare providers

Seek immediate emergency medical care if you have danger signs

8:26 ✈

September 4
11:59 AM   Edit
.ıl AT&T 🤶   11:59 AM
🔒 jamanetwork.com

JAMA Network

JAMA Neurology

the New...e-Ottawa Scale. Stud, ata were poo' using random-effects meta-analy is.

Main Outcomes and Measures The primary e posure was concussion and/or mild TBI, and th primary outcome was suicide. Secondary outcomes were suicide attempt and suicidal ideation.

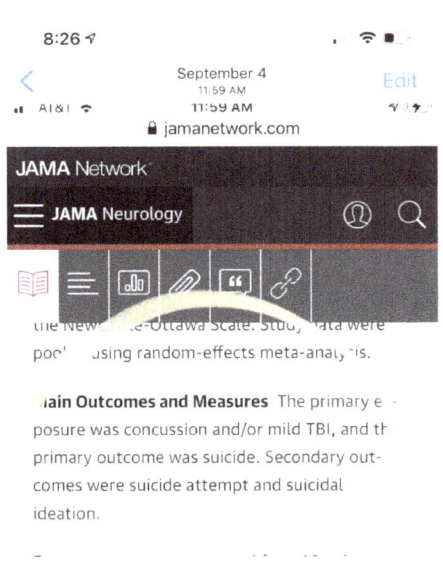

by Concussion Symptoms

Family and friends of those affected by a concussion or brain injury are some of the most loving, strong, amazing people. Living with someone who sustained a concussion can be incredibly stressful and exhausting. Being a caregiver is extremely difficult, even though you love the person you're caring for. It's frustrating because a concussion is an injury you can't see and is difficult to understand. The loved one didn't sustain the actual injury, but they can feel the effects of the injury on every level.

Did You Know?

A concussion is a real injury with real symptoms and impairments. After a concussion it can be very hard to understand and see the severity of these impairments. However, this does not make the impact on an individual any less real.

🔒 info.cognitivefxusa.com ↻

from "The Behavioral Inhibition System: A common cause of Post-Concussion Syndrome Depression," by Dr. Diane Spangler PhD

"Each of us has a behavioral activation system and a behavioral inhibition system. They monitor and reward (or suppress rewards for) our behavior. When the behavioral inhibition system gets triggered too often, depression can result.

How Behavioral Activation and Inhibition Work

You can think of the behavioral activation system as our brain's default setting. It makes us curious and eager to learn. It helps us feel rewarded for mastering a topic or experiencing something pleasurable. It's an important part of why we engage with the world and the people around us.

But in the background, the behavioral inhibition system is monitoring everything we do. It's watching out for loss, and it tells us whenever we've experienced a loss. And if we experience what it believes are too many losses, it pulls back on the reigns, dampening (or completely disrupting) the behavioral activation system.

... lingering post-concussion symptoms are strong activators of the behavioral inhibition system. And once that system is in control, it can prevent you from feeling pleasure or from feeling rewarded when you do something that used to make you feel satisfied in an effort to protect you from further loss. And when that inhibition system looks toward the future, all it sees is more loss, resulting in feelings of hopelessness...

Physical symptoms such as headaches, noise and light sensitivity, and fatigue, along with cognitive symptoms such as brain fog, memory problems, and poor concentration, make it difficult to work or attend school, engage in social outings, or even get some exercise. So recovery really can feel impossible.

The result? People who feel really crummy, experience multiple losses, and don't know how to get better. Often, our patients are surprised by how they feel. For examp e, sometimes parents will talk about how they think they must be monsters because they can't feel anything, even toward their kids. They struggle to care about anything and reveal how they never knew how terrible it could be to feel nothing or be so robotic.

It's so important to understand: There isn't something wrong with you for feeling this way. Your brain – specifically, your behavioral inhibition system – is just trying to protect you from further loss, and it's messing with your feelings in the process."

https://www.cognitivefxusa.com/blog/depression-after-concussion-and-post-concussion-syndrome

There is treatment and hope.

Emotional Symptoms

Depending on what part or parts of a person's brain are injured, the individual may experience significant behavioral and emotional changes.

The frontal lobe, for example, helps govern personality and impulsivity. If damaged, there might be no "braking mechanism" for self-control. A person may find he cannot control his anger or aggression. He may also make inappropriate comments to friends or strangers not realizing they are off color. Or the opposite might happen — someone's personality may become muted or seemingly emotionless. This is called "flat affect."

Resources and correlation of suicide and concussion aka Post concussion syndrome depression. Recent studies suggest a large majority of people don't fully recover from concussions, as was previously believed, which could lead to larger problems if left untreated.

CHECK YOUR SYMPTOMS   FIND A DOCTOR   FIND A DENTIST   CONNECT TO CARE   FIND LOWEST DRUG PRICES

HEALTH
A-Z

DRUGS &
SUPPLEMENTS

LIVING
HEALTHY

FAMILY &
PREGNANCY

NEWS &
EXPERTS

MENU⌄   Brain & Nervous System › News

Suicide Risk Higher in People with Brain Injury

FROM THE WEBMD ARCHIVES ⓘ

By Alan Mozes

HealthDay Reporter

TUESDAY, Aug. 14, 2018 (HealthDay News) -- Traumatic brain injury can trigger a daily struggle with headaches, neck pain, dizziness and thinking problems that may drive some to suicide, researchers report.

That risk more than triples in the first six months after a traumatic brain injury (TBI), and it stays significantly higher over the long term, a new Danish study suggests.

The finding is based on an exhaustive review of Danish health and death records. The data included all residents of Denmark who were at least 10 years old between 1980 and 2014 -- more than 7 million people in all, including almost 35,000 who died by suicide.

While the study shows that suicide among traumatic brain injury patients "is still a very rare event," according to lead author Trine Madsen, it also underscores that the impact of both mild and severe TBI on overall quality of life does appear to increase the risk.

https://www.webmd.com/brain/news/20180814/suicide-risk-higher-in-people-with-brain-injury

"Over time, a skull fracture without traumatic brain injury was linked to a nearly doubled suicide risk, and a mild TBI was tied to twice the suicide risk, the study found. A severe TBI injury, however, was associated with a 2.5 times increased suicide risk."

Health

1 person dies by suicide every 40 seconds, says WHO

f 🐦 ✉ 🔴 in

More people die by suicide every year than in war, the World Health Organization says

Thomson Reuters · Posted: Sep 09, 2019 1:54 PM ET | Last Updated: November 5, 2020

WHO's director-general Tedros Adhanom Ghebreyesus called on all countries to incorporate proven suicide prevention strategies into their national health programs. (Fabrice Coffrini/AFP/Getty Images)

https://www.cbc.ca/news/health/suicide-who-1.5276263

The World Health Organization states that "Suicide is a global public health issue. All ages, sexes and regions of the world are affected [and] each loss is one too many." "Suicide was the second leading cause of death among young people aged between 15 and 29, after road injury. Overall, close to 800,000 people die by suicide every year – more than are killed by malaria or breast cancer, or by war or homicide, the WHO said."

Stunned by the Research

I was stunned when I came across this article. The headline: "1 person dies by suicide every 40 seconds" had me horrified... our son was 1 of those persons!!

Doesn't this strike our world to want to know "why"??? How does one person in every 40 seconds take their own life???

Suicide is heard of but not discussed... until it happens to someone you know. And that's just what t's done to our family ~ "how" and "why" would our boy, who had everything to live for, be gone?!

This brings me to where I am today writing a book, sharing our life, our son's life, for the world to know he mattered. People have to know what causes suicides, what causes TBI/PCS, how do you end up burying your 24 year old son whose life had just begun, or others alike who I have mentioned in this section... They all had something in common ~ an injury, a concussion, a TBI!!!

Please take warning. Hear a heartbroken family's plea... awareness has to be made, so that lives can be saved!!

It is real.

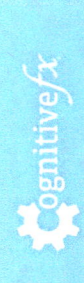

By: Dr. Alina Fong PhD Last Updated: May 24, 2022

Medically Reviewed by Dr. Jaycie Loewen   🖶 Print/Save as PDF

Suicidal Thoughts and Post-Concussion Syndrome: What Can You Do?

MENTAL HEALTH SUPPORT AFTER A BRAIN INJURY | DIAGNOSING PTSD SYMPTOMS | EDUCATIONAL RESOURCES | POST-CONCUSSION TREATMENT

Sustaining a traumatic brain injury can be a challenging experience. You probably felt angry, demoralized, helpless, and even hopeless in the days following your injury. For some people, these feelings eventually subside and disappear — but that didn't happen for you.

First, know that you are not alone: Up to 30% of concussion patients have long-lasting symptoms after their head injury. This is referred to as post-concussion syndrome (PCS) and may include symptoms such as brain fog, headaches, nausea, memory problems, and blurry vision.

Over 80% of our post-concussion syndrome patients report "personality changes" and mental health problems such as depression, post-traumatic stress disorder (PTSD), irritability, tearfulness, and more.

For some, the list of symptoms also includes suicidal thoughts. Suicidal ideation can be overwhelming and terrifying, or at the very least, unsettling. But it's important to know that these thoughts don't come from you; they are a side effect of your brain injury. The concussion you suffered can distort your thinking and emotions, so it becomes harder to see different solutions and find a way to move forward.

No matter how long you've had suicidal thoughts and feelings, this doesn't have to be a permanent state. With the right help, you can improve, just like the many other brain injury patients who have gotten help before you.

The crucial point here is to find the right help to **treat both your mental health and physical symptoms.** Treating your brain injury will go a long way to make you feel better. In the meantime, it's very important to address your suicidal thoughts.

Don't let anyone tell you that you can get over these thoughts by simply wishing them away or "toughening up." Depression and suicidal feelings can be treated by a doctor, just like diabetes or high blood pressure. Therapists, counselors, psychologists, and the treatment team at Cognitive FX can help you find solutions that otherwise may not be obvious to you.

In this article, we'll explain what could be causing your suicidal feelings and putting you at a risk of suicide, as well as suggest ways to cope and move forward with the right treatment. We cover:

- Why you may feel suicidal after a brain injury.
- What to do and what to avoid when you have suicidal feelings.
- How to get treated for post-concussion syndrome at Cognitive FX.
- Suggestions to help your recovery long-term.
- What friends and family can do to help.

Over 80% of our patients have experienced emotional symptoms after a concussion. Many of those symptoms resolve shortly after treatment at our clinic (although serious mental health issues such as depression and anxiety can take additional therapy to resolve). If you'd like to learn more about how we can help you, schedule a consultation.

Note: *Any data relating to brain function mentioned in this post is from our first generation fNCI scans. Gen 1 scans compared activation in various regions of the brain with a control database of healthy brains. Our clinic is now rolling out second-generation fNCI which looks both at the activation of individual brain regions and at the connections between brain regions. Results are interpreted and reported differently for Gen 2 than for Gen 1; reports will not look the same if you come into the clinic for treatment.*

Dr. David Clark, DC, helps people who've suffered Traumatic Brain Injuries and Concussions

Here is part of Dr. Clark's article in triangle TBI concussion:

"Let's face it... Life would be easier if you had a big scar, a cast or crutches. At least then your family and friends could SEE the damage your concussion did to you.

But that's not how things are. Your problem is not a broken bone. Your injury is deep inside your brain...in circuits that control your balance, mood and memory.

You can't talk to people about it because they look at you and they think...

'You look okay to me.
There's nothing wrong with you.'

People expect you to be exactly how you've always been. You're not. But you LOOK the same."

This article is a example of all the literature that is actually available. If you know and understand what you're looking for after your concussion and why you don't feel like you anymore, you might be able to find coping mechanisms to help you stay a survivor.

For our family, I found this information too late to save our son, but I share in hope that his voice is heard and others like him will get help before it's too late and their families will know and understand just what their loved one is going through.

People need to know sometimes your concussion doesn't just end because your physical appearance is looking better. PCS, TBI, and PTSD don't always get a proper diagnosis or care like injuries to the outer shell of our bodies do.

https://triangletbiconcussiondoctor.com/
Youtube: **https://www.youtube.com/c/DrDavidJClarkDC**

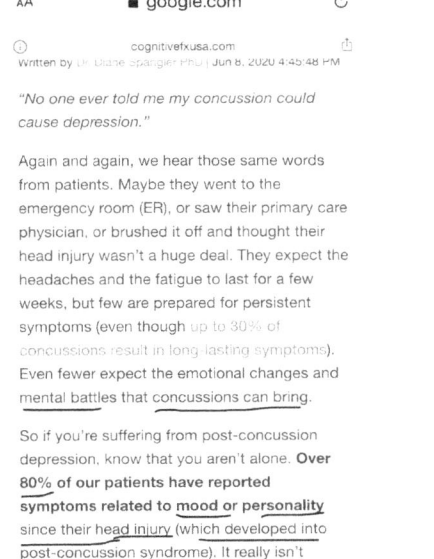

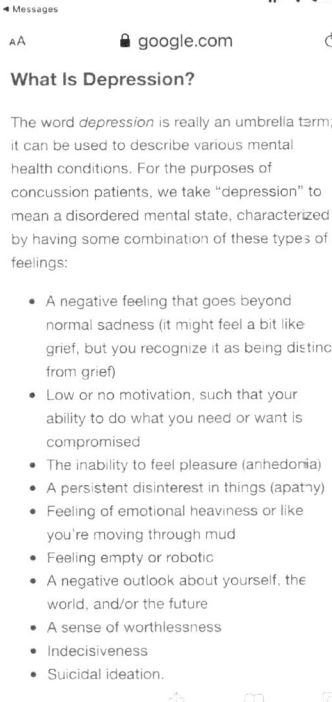

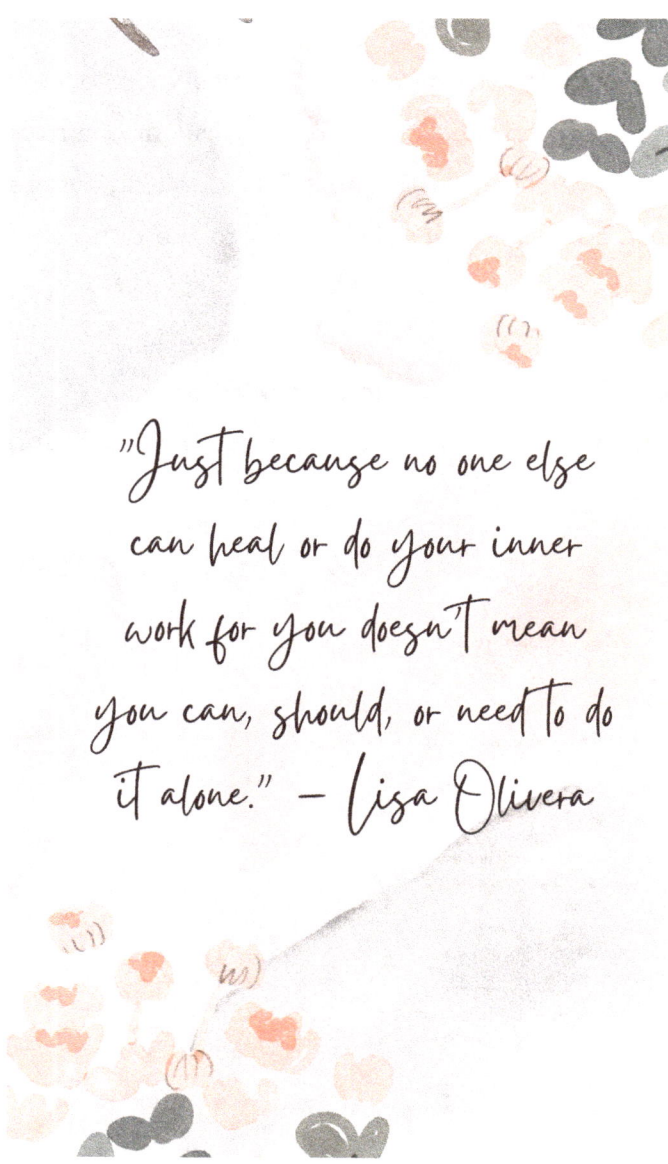

"Just because no one else can heal or do your inner work for you doesn't mean you can, should, or need to do it alone." — Lisa Olivera

Real World Examples

This terrible disease can afflict anyone. Usually it is only famous people who make the headlines. But take a look at just a few examples on the following pages to see the variety of people who are deeply affected by brain injury. IT IS REAL. There could be so many more examples in this book, but the point is to recognize what is happening and to offer hope, a listening ear, some perspective, refer to a mental health professional.

It's going to be hard, but hard doesn't mean impossible.

NEWS ✗ CULTURE ♪ MUSIC ♫ PODCASTS & SHOWS 🔍 SEARCH

NATIONAL

Olympic Cycling Medalist Kelly Catlin Dead At 23

March 11, 2019 · 4:51 PM ET

SASHA INGBER

Cyclist Kelly Catlin (left) with her U.S. teammates after they won team pursuit gold medals at the world championships in the Netherlands last year.

Peter Dejong/AP

Updated at 6:07 p.m. ET

Olympic cycling medalist Kelly Catlin died in her dorm at Stanford University last Thursday, an abrupt end to the 23-year-old's accolade-filled life.

https://www.npr.org/2019/03/11/702206945/olympic-cycling-medalist-kelly-catlin-dead-at-23

Along with her cycling team, Kelly Catlin won a silver medal during the 2016 Olympic Games in Rio de Janeiro. She suffered a concussion when she crashed on a slick road, just a few months before she took her own life – it was her second attempt. Her family said, "We didn't know about the racing thoughts and the obsessing over different things and the nightmares. We only knew about the headaches."

NATIONAL*POST

Post-mortem confirms Ty Pozzobon, rodeo star who died by suicide, had chronic brain injury

Chronic traumatic encephalopathy is only diagnosed post-mortem. It has been found most commonly in football players, other contact sport athletes and military personnel

Linda Givetash, The Canadian Press
Oct 10, 2017 • October 11, 2017 • 2 minute read

Ty Pozzobon of Merritt, British Colombia, makes the victory lap after taking the day money in the bull riding event during the Calgary Stampede rodeo in Calgary, Alta. on Wednesday July 9, 2014
PHOTO BY AL CHAREST/POSTMEDIA /Al Charest/Calgary Sun/QMI Agency

Neurologists from the University of Washington say a champion bull rider from British Columbia who died by suicide had a chronic brain condition.

https://www.theglobeandmail.com/sports/ty-pozzobon-concussion-bull-riding/article36842612/

A talent bull rider, Ty Pozzobon suffered over 13 concussions doing what he loved. Afflicted with chronic traumatic encephalopathy (CTE), "He was having balance issues and could not eat. He could not sleep and had trouble remembering things. He talked about being sad, and not knowing what he was going to do with his life. He was anxious and angry."

Manitoba

Post-concussion treatment, suicide prevention 'a team sport,' says lead researcher

f y ✉ ⊙ in

Suicide attempts common in post-concussion patients, says Dr. Charles Tator of the Canadian Concussion Centre

Sam Samson · CBC News · Posted: Mar 10, 2020 5:00 AM CT | Last Updated: March 10, 2020

Taylor Pryor, 21, died by suicide a year after suffering from a concussion while playing soccer. (Taylor Pryor/Facebook)

A leading concussion expert says suicide attempts are much more common among people suffering from concussions than many realize, but are preventable if patients get the proper care.

https://www.cbc.ca/news/canada/manitoba/suicide-post-concussion-research-taylor-pryor-winnipeg-1.5491646

Taylor Pryor suffered a concussion during a soccer game, just one year before she took her own life. "Pryor's family says her demeanour drastically changed after the concussion. She went from being a motivated university student to suddenly exhibiting severe post-concussion syndromes like anger, lethargy and sensitivity to light. Pryor attempted suicide at least 22 times before her death."

OLYMPICS

U.S. Olympic bobsledder Pavle Jovanovic dies by suicide at 43

 By Cindy Boren

May 11, 2020 at 10:00 a.m. EDT

Pavle Jovanovic, who died May 3, in a 2005 photo (Ed Andrieski/AP)

https://www.washingtonpost.com/sports/2020/05/11/us-olympic-bobsledder-pavle-jovanovic-dies-by-suicide-age-43/

Pavle Jovanovic was a well loved and respected athlete, who inspired his teammates and many others. His suicide in 2020 made him the second Olympic bobsledder to have died in three years, the other being his former teammate Steven Holcomb, a celebrated medalist, who was open about his depression. In a social media post, another one of Jovanovic's former teammates posted that this was the sixth death of Olympic athletes he'd competed with.

All about brain injury and PTSD

Life After Brain Injury: My Struggle with Depression

Brandon Blake and Michelle Kauffman share how they worked to address challenges they faced with depression after experiencing a brain injury.

https://www.brainline.org/video/life-after-brain-injury-my-struggle-depression

Brandon Blake is a TBI/PCS survivor who sustained a very traumatic accident while in his commute home from work. He describes brain injury like, "being on an unfamiliar roller coaster blind folded, you don't know what's happening and you never know when it's going to stop!"

He says in this video: "Any listener who is listening right now, who may be struggling with their recovery and brain injury, or know somebody who is, I would say this: treat recovery. If you're going through this, treat it like your full time job. Like, that's it. I had to put my life on hold as I knew it, my career as a preschool teacher on hold, my work, being a musician in a band and playing gigs out, out around town, on hold, doing massive art pieces on hold, everything I loved on hold. My job now was my brain. I think I had recovery as my full time job for the first two and a half years."

The terrifying link between concussions and suicide

By Erin Blakemore

February 22, 2016 at 9:00 a.m. EST

Bennet Omalu is pictured on the red carpet on Dec. 9 for a screening of the movie, "Concussion." Omalu is credited with helping bring the dangers of concussions in sports into the public spotlight. (Sarah L. Voisin/The Washington Post)

https://www.washingtonpost.com/news/to-your-health/wp/2016/02/22/the-terrfying-link-between-concussions-and-suicide/

In the study discussed in this article, research was done on 235,000 people. "Rather than focus on athletes or people who were hospitalized for days or weeks after head injuries, they looked at ordinary people who had concussions but did not sustain severe brain injury. The researchers matched those whose official death certificates listed suicide with their medical history over a 20-year period. They found a suicide rate of 31 deaths per 100,000 patients – three times the population norm. The mean time between a mild concussion and suicide was 5.7 years, and each additiona concussion raised suicide risk."

Donald Redelmeier, a practicing physician and professor of medicine who led the study says, "Look after your brain. People just don't take concussions seriously."

Resources

There are many resources included in this book. Most of them were what I found during my search to understand what happened to Seth. Here are a few websites that might be very helpful to you.

With social media there's a world of resources at your fingertips including post concussion groups through facebook groups... You are more than your injury, knowing what to search is key and will help you realize you are not alone, just as our son, your life too matters!

National Suicide Hotline
1-800-273-8255
The word suicide should not be so taboo ~ you know you better than anyone. Get to the root cause of why you feel your life isn't worth living. I can give you 10,000,000 reasons why it is. Please stay, be here tomorrow.

Cognitive FX
1-385-375-8590
info@cognitivefxusa.com
It also includes Cognitive Fx, a medical facility in Utah that specializes in TBI/PCS depression syndrome. I've shared a few of their resources on earlier pages. Prayers this finds you and anyone else who may be in need of answers before it's too late.

National Institute of Mental Health
1-866-615-6464
For general information about depression: http://www.nimh.nih.gov/health/topics/depression/index.shtml

More education about post concussion (hashtags)
#postconcussionsyndromedepression
#concussioncommunity
#beheretomorrow

About the Author

Laura Kimbro is not an expert on brain injuries, concussions, or anything health related for that matter. She is "just" a mom who wants others to be aware of what can happen as a result of an accident. She sits in a hard place in reliving the death of her son for the sake of bringing awareness to this issue in hopes that others will find the help they need in their time of crisis. She did not want this responsibility, but takes it on in order to bring Seth's voice to as many ears as possible. To give light to the darkness and share hope for the future.

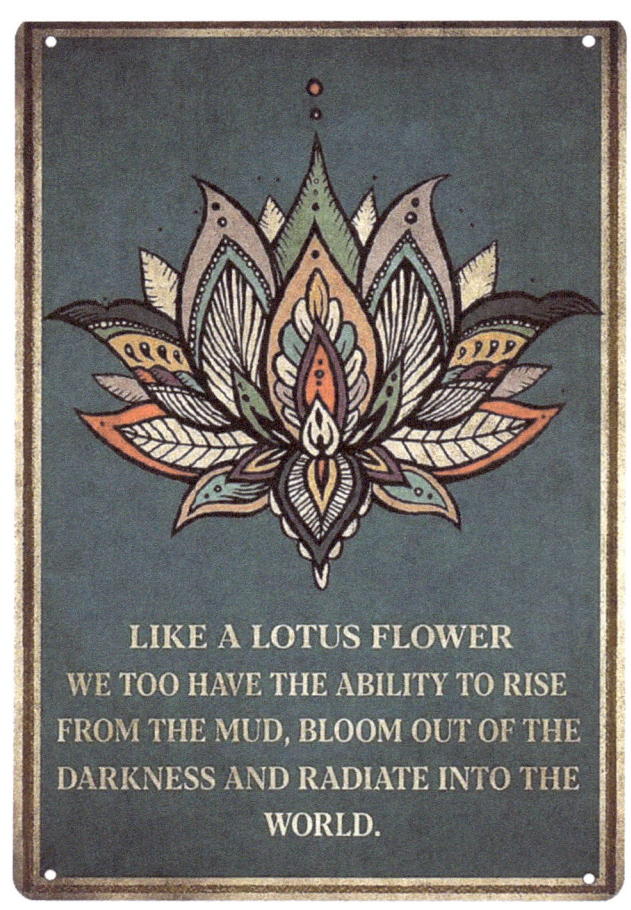

www.ingramcontent.com/pod-product-compliance
Lightning Source LLC
Chambersburg PA
CBHW071721140626
46557CB00012B/1201